Frames of Mind

MOTIVATION ACCORDING TO KABBALAH

The Judaism and Modern Times Series

FRAMES OF MIND

MOTIVATION ACCORDING TO KABBALAH

by

Rabbi Yitzchak Ginsburgh

ג	ל	ע	י	נ	י
ו	א	ב	י	ט	ה
נ	פ	ל	א	ו	ת
מ	ת	ו	ר	ת	ר

Gal Einai

Jerusalem • New York

THE JUDAISM AND MODERN TIMES SERIES

FRAMES OF MIND

MOTIVATION ACCORDING TO KABBALAH

Rabbi Yitzchak Ginsburgh

Edited by Yonatan Gordon

Printed in the United States of America and Israel
First Edition

For information:

Israel: GAL EINAI
          PO Box 1015
          Kfar Chabad 60840
          tel. (in Israel): 1-700-700-966
          tel. (from abroad): 972-3-9608008

email: books@inner.org

Web: www.inner.org
Twitter: @RabbiGinsburgh

Printed with the support of the Torah Institute of Yeshivat Od Yosef Chai.

Layout: David Hillel
Cover design: Batsheva Levinson

ISBN: 978-965-7146-79-8

TABLE OF CONTENTS

Editor's Note

The teaching that would eventually become this book was first presented by Rabbi Ginsburgh as an addendum to a class about the Seven Weeks of Consolation which follow Tisha B'Av—the 9th day of the Hebrew month of Av—the most tragic day of the Hebrew calendar when the Holy Temple in Jerusalem was twice destroyed.

The class was given at the Hebrew University of Jerusalem on the 11th of Av, 5773 (July 18, 2013) where Rabbi Ginsburgh headlined the annual celebration of course completion at Torat HaNefesh, a school of Jewish psychology which operates under his direction. The atmosphere at the gathering was quite lively, with the popular Halev Ve'HaMa'ayan klezmer band performing during the musical intermissions. Then the participants—chiefly students who are training to become counselors according to the approach first laid out by the 18th century founder of the Chassidic Movement, the Ba'al Shem Tov—settled down for the culminating event: Rabbi Ginsburgh's address.

When Rabbi Ginsburgh began speaking, he gave no indication of the topic that he would introduce later. He spoke about the Seven Weeks of Consolation and the power of unconditional love of one person for another. What followed next came as a complete surprise and, for me, it served as an introduction to the most important of the ideas underpinning the teachings presented in this book.

Relating back to a statement he made earlier in the class, that the Hebrew word for "consolation"— *nechamah* (נֶחָמָה)—also means "change of mind," Rabbi Ginsburgh quoted a verse from the First Book of Samuel: "The Eternal of Israel does not deceive and does not change His mind, for He is not a man to change His mind."[1] Then he noted that, despite this declaration, the Talmudic sages held that God did indeed change His mind when He created the world. God had intended to create the world with a measure of strict justice but, instead, He created it with a measure of compassion.[2] "So which is it?" Rabbi Ginsburgh asked, "Does God change His mind, or doesn't He?"

His answer contained a most amazing idea—that, when it comes to God, both can be true simultaneously. God can be non-changing (fixed) and God can be changing (growth-oriented) all the time. For the Divine, these two dynamics can, and do, exist together in the same moment.

For us human beings who are bound by time and space, in order to traverse from one level of understanding to the next, higher level of understanding, our entire conceptual scheme needs to be open to reversing itself from one moment to the next. But the same does not hold for the Almighty, who does not have our limitations. God is both changing and non-changing at the same time. Indeed, what is *non-changing* is that in every split second, there is a new Divine light that enables creation to continually change or proceed from one level of understanding to the next.

To the reader first being introduced to this topic the difference between non-changing and changing, fixed and growth mindsets, may not be clear. The reader could reasonably ask: If even non-changing behavior—as essentially expressed in the behavior of God Himself—is constantly being revealed at every moment, then maybe those things that we perceive as fixed, are not fixed at all?

The fascinating answer, and how it is understood by Kabbalah, is the subject of the pages that follow.

A Second Class

Shortly after the initial mindsets material was presented during the Torat HaNefesh address, a class was held on the 29th of Av, 5773 (August 5th, 2013) in Kfar Chabad. This time the focus of the entire class was on mindsets, and much of this book was derived and adapted from the transcript of that second class.

Writing Conventions

Every effort was made to make the concepts presented here accessible to those readers not familiar with Kabbalistic ideas or terminology. As well, the advanced student was kept in mind and wherever possible original Hebrew words and phrases have been included.

Differing from our previous books, whenever a verse refers to more than one name of God—the ineffable four-letter name, *Havayah* (יְהוה) and the common reference to the Almighty, *Elokim* (אֱלֹהִים)—we transliterated both. However, whenever a verse refers to only one name of God, we simply used "God" to ease with reading of the text.

When the word "Torah" is used, it is an inclusive term used to connote the Five Books of Moses, the Prophets, and/or the Scriptures—referred in Hebrew as the *Tanach* (תנ״ך) the acronym of Torah (תּוֹרָה, i.e., the Five Books of Moses), *Nevi'im* (נְבִיאִים, i.e., the Prophets), and *Ketuvim* (כְּתוּבִים, i.e., the Writings/Scriptures).

Acknowledgements

I would like to thank Rabbi Moshe Genuth for transcribing and annotating the original classes given by Rabbi Ginsburgh, my wife Hila for her endless encouragement, and Mrs. Rachel Gordon and Mrs. Uriela Sagiv for their editorial assistance.

May the Almighty help that we should each be able to carry out our purpose in life, properly balanced between growth and fixed mindsets.

Yonatan Gordon

Migdal Eder (Bat Ayin), a community in the Land of Israel, founded by Rabbi Ginsburgh in 5749 (1989).

14 Tevet, 5774

INTRODUCTION

The concept of "mindset" is a hot topic in psychology today. It was first made popular by the Stanford University professor, Dr. Carol S. Dweck, a well-known innovator in the field of human behavior and motivation, with the publication of *Mindset: The New Psychology of Success*.[1]

In this ground-breaking book, Dr. Dweck introduced the idea of a "fixed mindset" versus a "growth mindset" and explained how more than 35 years of research have led her to the conclusion that beliefs which people hold about their intelligence, talent and abilities make a world of difference to what extent they are able to succeed in life.

Those who believe that their successes are due to innate or natural abilities have a "fixed mindset," she said. Those who believe that their successes come as the result of effort, hard work and the willingness to overcome challenges and obstacles in the way have a "growth mindset." As she put it:

> In a fixed mindset, students believe their basic abilities, their intelligence, their talents, are just fixed traits. They have a certain amount and

that's that, and then their goal becomes to look smart all the time and never look dumb. In a growth mindset students understand that their talents and abilities can be developed through effort, good teaching and persistence. They don't necessarily think everyone's the same or anyone can be Einstein, but they believe everyone can get smarter if they work at it.[2]

Her research has also shown that students with a growth mindset do better at school, especially when difficulties are encountered. At first both fixed and growth students may appear very similar in their attendance, grades and general class participation. But when there are surprises—such as an extraordinarily difficult test, or missed school days— students with a growth mindset are better able to overcome these hurdles, and their growth mindset becomes the model for future successes as well.

Reinforcing Dr. Dweck's ideas, Melbourne University professor, Dr. John Hattie, conducted a 15-year study on learning and achievement for school-aged children, which he presents in his book *Visible Learning: A Synthesis of Over 800 Meta-Analyses Relating to Achievement*. There he writes that "the willingness to invest in learning, to gain a reputation as a learner, and to show openness to experiences are the key dispositional factors that relate to achievement."[3]

When students focus on learning, instead of looking smart or other outward appearances, their world of study begins to open before them. If before they were afraid to raise their hand in class for fear of appearing silly, when properly inculcated with a growth mindset, these students are more willing to risk backlash from peers and participate in class discussions. Since the focus is on the pursuit of knowledge instead of prestige, growth mindsets are more likely to propose even creative or out-of-the-box ideas instead of staying silent.

According to Dr. Hattie, teachers should first teach their students to have the right mindset. Only once the importance of personal growth and effort are firmly inculcated in the students' minds and hearts should teachers begin to teach.

Education in the Jewish Tradition

Of course, the Jewish tradition has always emphasized education and considered it nothing less than a religious duty. The result was that in the ancient world—where literacy was a scant 5 percent[4]—Jews were almost fully literate. In his *The*

Jewish Contribution to Civilization, historian Cecil Roth confirms:

> [Among the Jews] illiteracy was almost unknown ... The Jews, as a result of their respect for the written code of religious law, were the first of all people to institute an elementary school system.[5]

So important was this obligation to educate that Rabbi Joshua Ben Gamla, high priest in the 1st century CE, ordained that "teachers of young children should be appointed in each district and each town and that children should enter school at age six or seven."[6] The famed 12th century Jewish philosopher, Maimonides, put it even more strongly:

> Teachers shall be appointed for the children in every country, province and city. If a city does not have a school, the people of the city shall be excommunicated until they get teachers for the children. If they don't, the city shall be destroyed, because the world exists only because of the breath of children studying.[7]

Of course, no Jewish court ever ordered a community to be destroyed for lack of a school, because virtually every Jewish community had free public education long before anyone else thought of it.

As a result, the Jews became the first fully literate nation in history and earned for themselves the title: "the People of the Book." But even more than that, they always were "the People *for* the Book," meaning that the focus of Jewish education always was the Book—the Torah—the blueprint for living a moral and ethical life in accordance with God's commandments. Thus it is the Jewish view that one is never free to desist from the task of toiling in education and growth through Torah. [8]

Education is such a central theme in Judaism that the educational components of holidays and observances are often mandated by Jewish law. For example: The *Haggadah* that is read on Passover was formulated to arouse the questions and curiosity of the children sitting at the table. The word Chanukah (חֲנוּכָּה) shares the same Hebrew word root as the word for "education"—*chinuch* (חִנּוּךְ). During Purim, we recall the heroism of the 22,000 young children gathered by Mordechai in Shushan to learn Torah and pray for God's mercy in response to the threat of death hanging over the Jewish people—to name just a few of a great many other examples.

This Jewish emphasis on education means that any Jewish parent, teacher or student is interested in anything that will improve and inspire learning. But is this latest theory compatible with Judaism or not? Is it worth studying and adapting to the Torah lifestyle?

The answer is yes. Indeed, Dr. Dweck's theory of growth and fixed mindset provides a fresh take on classic Jewish teachings and Kabbalistic concepts. And that brings us to the purpose of this book—to introduce the reader to the mystical approach to motivation.

We all know how important motivation is in all types of human endeavor. Let's say we pick up a book—it looks interesting, inspiring, and beneficial even, but then something happens, and we put it down. That something is a distraction. The antidote is motivation.

While our lives appear to be moving at an ever increasing pace, we risk an experience known as the vertigo of modernism. With so much happening all around, amidst the dizzying pace of progress and change, how do we keep our focus and maintain our motivation?

As we struggle to gain our foothold in the world of the present, we need to first frame our modern-day challenges and obstacles in light of the experiences of the past. But even as we hold onto the past, we also need to set our sights on the future. Like a sprinter or archer who first withdraws in order to spring forward, we withdraw to the ancient source of motivation in order to propel ourselves farther forward.

In synthesizing ancient and modern ideas, *Frames of Mind* demonstrates how we can reach our goals faster and arrive closer to the target than we ever thought possible.

1

THE RIGHT MINDSET

Praising Children to Succeed

An overabundance of research shows that the key to success, to becoming a fully contributing member of society, to achieving one's highest potential, is having the right mindset. According to Dr. Dweck's particular theory, both educators and parents are entrusted with a hefty responsibility. It is up to them to inculcate a growth mindset in children from a very young age.

But how are teachers and parents to do this? How are they to convince their students and children of the importance of effort, growth and self-improvement?

Dr. Dweck makes a case for praise as the primary tool for fostering a growth mindset. But she strongly differentiates between praising innate traits (such as intelligence for example) and praising "the process" a student uses to overcome difficulties (such as effort or strategy). She states that when educators praise the process, students are better encouraged to take on challenges in the future.

That would seem to be a given. But before we begin to discuss the importance of praise, let us first ask a fundamental question: If the intention is to encourage growth, then isn't praise counterproductive? Doesn't praise lead to a sense of self-satisfaction and a feeling that one may now rest on one's laurels?

While a growth-minded child will probably still plow forward, praise should be delivered in such a form that it will motivate one and all to do more. Even those children who seem self-motivated should be presented with a path ahead of them that further encourages their ambition. And this is where the method of praise becomes so important.

A fundamental teaching of the Chassidic Movement (Chassidut) is that praise is good as long as it encourages latent talents, abilities or traits to surface.

As an example, let us imagine two students named David and Sol. Sol is very angry with David and has come to David's dormitory to tell him off. David opens the door, and before Sol can launch into his diatribe, he calls out to his friends, "Hey fellows, look who is here—Sol, the nicest guy in my class!" Having been praised for being very nice, Sol is disarmed. And even if a moment before he had felt like punching David in the nose, he cannot help but smile and, instead of throwing a punch, he might actually throw both arms around David in greeting. This is what Chassidic literature calls "revealing the attribute of loving-kindness," which is also known as *chesed*, and which is one of the deep and hidden properties of the soul that can rise to the surface as a result of praise.

But praise is not always the answer. The *Tanya*—an 18th century book of Chassidic mysticism penned by Rabbi Schnuer Zalman of Liadi—instructs when to give praise and how to apply it, but together with this, it also instructs when to give rebuke and the best way to do so.[1]

If one child has his fist raised against another, a good teacher knows that this is not the proper time to praise the child with the raised fist! The teacher has to grab the child's hand or yell at him. Afterwards, the teacher must tell the child that, even though he was prevented from hitting, the act of raising his hand against another is still a transgression. We learn this from the Torah account—related in the Book of Exodus—of the two Hebrew men whom Moses saw quarreling; Moses called the one who raised his hand "wicked." Even though he didn't actually strike his friend, Moses still called him wicked.[2] In our example then, even if one child doesn't actually come to hit the other, the teacher must still correct him.

Unlike rebuke which is sometimes necessary in the heat of a fight, praise must precede such events as preventative medicine. If a child has the tendency to hit other children, a good teacher should always be on the lookout for a proper time to emphasize his positive qualities so that he won't hit the next time. As has been well documented, one of the underlying causes for one kid to bully another is low self-esteem. So while a teacher can never overlook or encourage the actual wrongdoing, praise will go a long way in raising the child's self-esteem and eradicating (or at least lessening) the need to rebuke.

Thus praise is the solution to many problems and, according to Dr. Dweck, the key to developing a growth mindset which, in turn, is the key to success. She maintains that if we learn how to praise people (especially children) correctly, we will help them to be more successful in life.[3]

Now, all that seems like basic common sense even if the nomenclature—fixed and growth mindsets—is novel. Simply put: If you have a growth mindset, you are most likely to succeed, but if you have a fixed mindset, your chances for being successful are not as good in the long run. So what makes this seemingly intuitive theory appear to be something so innovative?

Our task in this book is to uncover the conceptual basis for the mindset theory in the Torah. By doing so, we will be able to not only reveal what the point of attraction is—the idea that drew hundreds of thousands to read about this theory to begin with— but also to further expound upon the core concepts behind it.

New Nomenclature

While it is true that recent publication dates don't necessarily make the content any more recent, there *is* something that new books bring to the mix—and that is (as in the case of the Dweck book) new nomenclature.

This is to be expected. A famous Chassidic story recounts the process of how every few generations new names appear for the "good inclination" (*yetzer*

tov—יֵצֶר טוֹב) and the "evil inclination" (*yetzer hara*—
יֵצֶר הָרָע):

A chassid once came to Rabbi Dov Ber, son of
Rabbi Schneur Zalman and the second Rebbe of
Chabad, to ask for advice on how to rectify his
sense of being. The Rebbe replied, "Do you
even know what a sense of being is?" Of course,
the chassid didn't dare to answer. The Rebbe
then began to tell him at length the story of
Adam in Gan Eden, and the division of roles
that God gave out to the side of holiness and the
other side. Each one had to disseminate their
own philosophy. One that "there is nothing else
beside Him" and the other that "God has
forsaken the world". The "other side" answered
God that theirs is an impossible task, because
no one will believe them. God calmed them
down and told them not to worry, because He
will disguise them in the disguise of a serpent
and they will be successful. After Adam had
sinned the serpent came to God and told Him
that now his case was lost, because now
everyone knows him and no one will ever listen
to him again. God reassured him that He would
again change his disguise and changed his
name to the Angel of Death. That endured until

the time of Abraham, but once Abraham had overcome him, he once again came to God and God changed his name to the evil inclination and then again to Satan (as in the sages' legend of how it was Satan who tried to interfere on the way to the Binding of Isaac). This endured until the Giving of the Torah when God changed it to the animal soul and then again to the arrogance of Torah scholars. This prospered until the time of the Ba'al Shem Tov, who annihilated arrogance [being] altogether. The Torah scholars during the time of the Ba'al Shem Tov wanted "to be somebody;" they wanted to feel that they have being. What now? Now it's called "a sense of being." Then the Rebbe turned to him and said that it's all one.

The sages say that there are seven names-synonyms for the evil inclination in the Torah,[4] and likewise throughout the course of history it has changed its name seven times: the Primordial Snake (*nachash hakadmoni*—נָחָשׁ הַקַּדְמוֹנִי), the Angel of Death (*malach hamavet*—מַלְאַךְ הַמָּוֶת), the evil inclination (*yetzer hara*—יֵצֶר הָרָע), the Satan (שָׂטָן), the animal soul (*nefesh habahamit*—נֶפֶשׁ הַבַּהֲמִית), "being" (*yeshut*—יֵשׁוּת), and "a sense of being" (*hargashat hayesh*—הַרְגָּשַׁת הַיֵּשׁ). The last has a strong connection with the first.[5]

Indeed in the 18th century, Rabbi Schneur Zalman of Liadi, the founder of the Chabad Chassidic Movement—dubbed them the "animal soul" (*nefesh behamit*—נֶפֶשׁ הַבְּהֵמִית) and the "Divine soul" (*nefesh elokit*—נֶפֶשׁ אֱלוֹקִית). Later, Chassidic literature refers to them as "egocentricity" (*yeshut*—יֵשׁוּת) and "selflessness" (*bitul*—בְּטוּל).

And so, the first novelty that stems from an otherwise intuitive theory is that we now have two new names for these central components of human psychology—the good and evil inclinations—to work with! Instead of calling them the good and evil inclinations, we can now refer to them as the growth and fixed mindsets. This fact alone merits the theory becoming popular.[6]

To examine the theory of mindsets further, let us look at a diagram that Dweck uses:

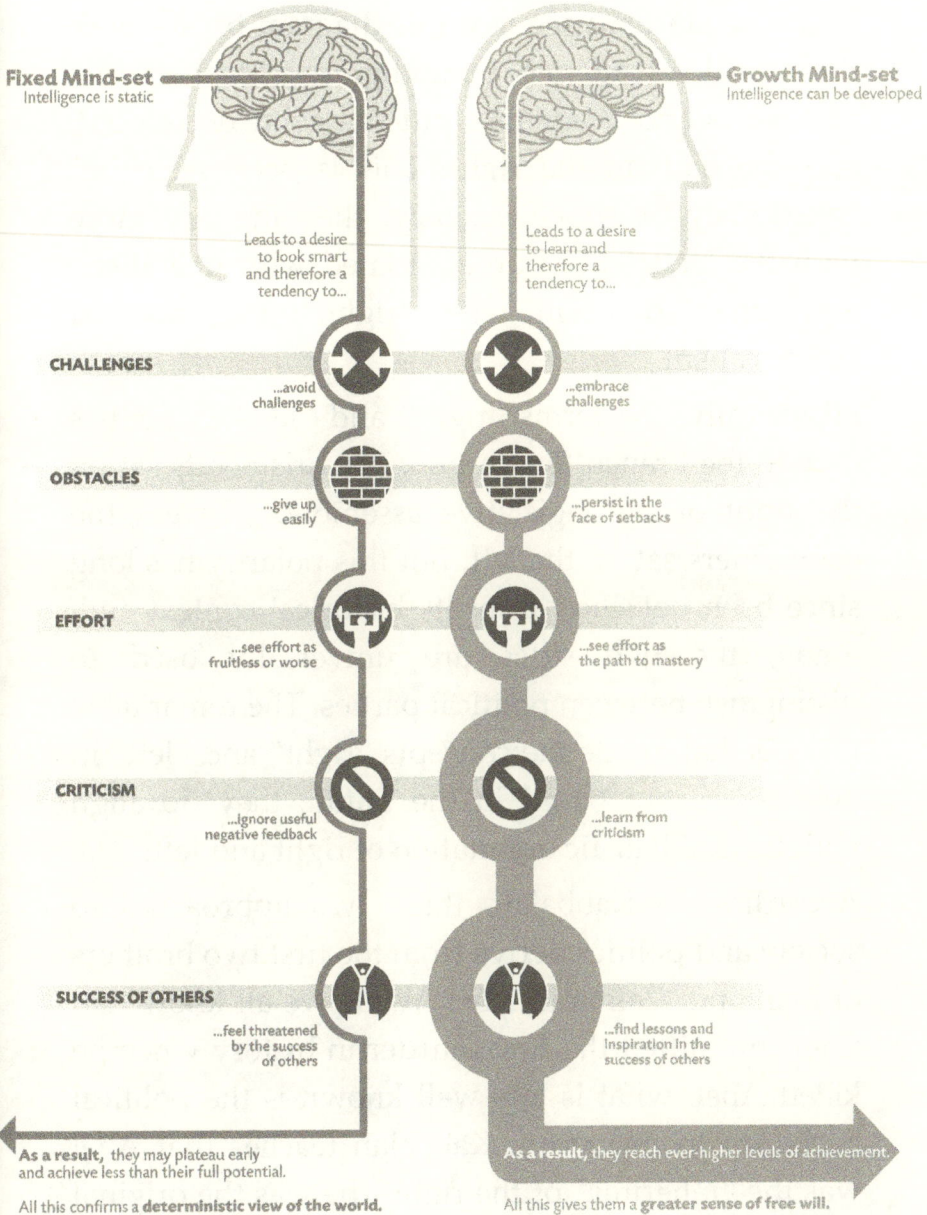

Fixed Mind-set
Intelligence is static

Growth Mind-set
Intelligence can be developed

Leads to a desire
to look smart
and therefore a
tendency to...

Leads to a desire
to learn and
therefore a
tendency to...

CHALLENGES

...avoid
challenges

...embrace
challenges

OBSTACLES

...give up
easily

...persist in the
face of setbacks

EFFORT

...see effort as
fruitless or worse

...see effort as
the path to mastery

CRITICISM

...ignore useful
negative feedback

...learn from
criticism

SUCCESS OF OTHERS

...feel threatened
by the success
of others

...find lessons and
inspiration in the
success of others

As a result, they may plateau early
and achieve less than their full potential.

All this confirms a **deterministic view of the world.**

As a result, they reach ever-higher levels of achievement.

All this gives them a **greater sense of free will.**

GRAPHIC BY NIGEL HOLMES

From the start we see that this diagram breaks with traditional academic paradigms. Most often, professors and academics put the good on the left, and the bad on the right. This is because, either consciously or subconsciously, they identify more with the "left," the side associated with liberalism, than they do with the "right," the side of conservatism.

Historically, the terms "right" and "left" in politics date to the French Revolution. The aristocrats sat on the right of the legislative assembly, whereas the commoners sat on the left. But this polarity has long since been detached from its historical context and, today, the two sides are universally used to distinguish between political parties. The remarkable thing is that, while the concepts "right" and "left" in politics are not based in the Torah, they do align with the Kabbalistic orientation of right and left.

According to Kabbalah, these two approaches to society and politics derive from the first two brothers of mankind: Cain and Abel. While we all know that Cain committed the first murder in history when he killed Abel, what is less well known is the political backdrop to this story. Kabbalah teaches that Abel was the "inheritor" of the right—he was the original rightist—whereas Cain was the original leftist. Cain was the "down-to-earth" brother who farmed the land, and Abel was the flighty idealist who roamed the fields looking after his sheep and conversing with God.[7] Although Abel led a more spiritual lifestyle, in the end, he fell victim to his more materialistically-minded brother.

In addition to Cain and Abel being the participants of the first left-right political contest, it is also taught in Kabbalah that the left is more prone to the evil inclination, while the right is more prone to the good inclination. This fits well with the Dweck's theory as mapped out in her diagram. Here, the left side describes the negative tendencies of the fixed mindset, and the right describes the positive tendencies of the growth mindset.

Kabbalistically speaking, our ultimate aim is to transform the left (or at least some of it) into the right. In this case, it means taking someone with a fixed mindset and teaching that person how to adopt a growth mindset. Thus, Dweck's surprising decision to break with convention and put the good on the right side and the bad on the left helps us align Kabbalistic ideas with hers, and this we shall now proceed to do.

Dweck's Diagram Reinterpreted

Dweck's premise is that the fixed mindset assumes all talent to be innate. What you were born with is what you have. You were either a born genius or not. (This accords with the Yiddish aphorism that "No one is going to put a new head on you!")

On the other hand, the growth mindset assumes that you can always improve and that even your IQ can increase, because if you work hard, you can develop new cells in your brain. This doesn't mean that you can grow infinitely, nor that you can become an Einstein or a Mozart (for which you would require a totally new head), but you are not fixed—you can always improve. To the growth mindset, the world is not a deterministic place. A growth mindset believes strongly in free will, for through free will, you can progress far beyond your native character traits. But a fixed mindset says that you're stuck. What you were dealt at birth is what you have.

As Dweck begins to map out the differences between the growth and fixed mindsets, it is not immediately clear which side is good, and which side is bad. Yes, she says that the fixed mindset avoids challenges, but sometimes it is better to give up than to hit your head against a brick wall. And, even beyond that, sometimes surrendering can be the most heroic action.

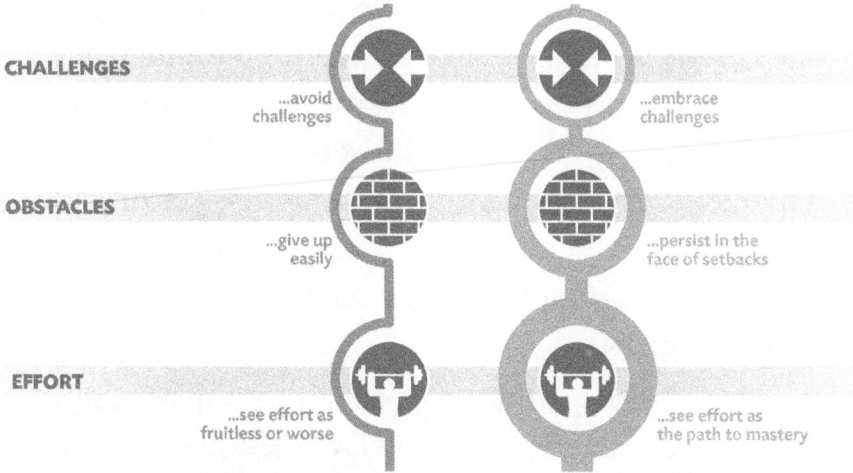

CHALLENGES
...avoid challenges
...embrace challenges

OBSTACLES
...give up easily
...persist in the face of setbacks

EFFORT
...see effort as fruitless or worse
...see effort as the path to mastery

The real difference between the growth and fixed mindsets comes into view in the third stage which refers to effort. Effort has only positive connotations and it is something which everyone should be capable of. Those people who don't expend effort in our society are seen as lazy. From Dweck's point of view, it could very well be that such people have been conditioned to believe that they were born smart and all they need do is let everyone else know how smart they are. Or that they were born lucky, and all they need do is wave the "winning lottery ticket" proudly in the air. Following this reasoning, it is primarily a fixed *self-image* that leads a person to adopt a fixed mindset.

Of course, there are plenty of people who realize that they have a higher-than-average native intelligence who still work hard to learn even more. These people have growth mindsets however. What separates the brilliant fixed mindset from the brilliant growth mindset is that the fixed mindset cares more about outer impressions than about their ability to grow.

In Chassidut, this is called "superficiality" (*hitzoniyut*—חִיצוֹנִיּוּת). And Dweck demonstrates where superficiality in adults originates.

Most of her research was conducted with children in school, and she has reached the conclusion that it is crucial to inculcate a growth mindset from a very young age. This is a very Jewish idea, as the *Ethics of the Fathers* states:

> Elisha ben Avuyah said: "One who learns as a child, what is he like? Like ink written on new paper. One who learns as an old man, what is he like? Like ink written on blotted paper." Rabbi Yose bar Yehudah of Kfar HaBavli said: "One who learns from the young, what is he like? Like one who eats unripe grapes and drinks wine directly from the press. One who

learns from the elders, what is he like? Like one who eats ripe grapes and drinks vintage wine." Rabbi Meir said: "Do not pay attention to the jar, but its contents. There are new jars full of vintage wine and old jars that do not contain even new wine."[8]

Although growth-minded children will try and fail, try and fail, over and over (and occasionally try and succeed), they will view each apparent setback as a springboard to eventual success. When it comes to challenges, the motto of the growth mindset individual—whether consciously stated or subconsciously understood—is that if you're afraid to fail, you will never succeed.

Similarly, if children are afraid of obstacles, then they will run away from them, or try to avoid them. But if they have a growth mindset, then they will persist. In the face of setbacks, they will keep pushing forward.

This is what really surprised Dweck—that some children naturally feel this way! Some children naturally realize that failure is part of the game, or the process of growing up. It came as a great discovery for Dweck that some children never understood that there is another way of seeing failure—that it could be interpreted as something negative. For to them, it never was. These children did not equate failure with failure but only with magnified challenge.

In Chassidut, this is called "descent for the purpose of ascent" (yeridah tzorech aliyah—יְרִידָה צוֹרֶךְ עֲלִיָּה). Rebbe Nachman of Breslov—the 18th century founder of the Breslover Chassidic sect—goes further in describing this frame of mind as "the essence of descent is ascent" (yeridah tachlit aliyah—יְרִידָה תַּכְלִית עֲלִיָּה). People who think this way don't ever think they are descending because, to them, the descent is part of the ascent—like a mountain climber who sometimes must descend to cross a chasm but all the while he is climbing the mountain.

The Talmud states: "A person only properly understands the words of the Torah after stumbling over them."[9] We first make a mistake or experience failure in the learning process, and only then do we come to the proper understanding. Interestingly, the root in Hebrew for "failure" (keshel—כֶּשֶׁל) is a permutation of the word for "intelligence" (sechel—שֵׂכֶל). Just as we rearrange the letters that spell failure to arrive at intelligence, we rearrange the psychological components that produced failure to reach success.

Frowning vs. Smiling

There is an important lesson that comes from this. If children don't see their teachers and parents frowning at them when they fail, then they won't know the usefulness of a frown as an educational tool.

Although a teacher would always prefer to smile in order to motivate the student, it is sometimes better to frown. It should be noted that, even when he or she is frowning, the teacher should be just as loving and caring on the inside. Indeed, this is how God conducts the world.

God frowns, so to speak, when He allows upsetting things to happen to us, which are eventually revealed as being for our good and betterment. So, too, a parent or a teacher can't always say "yes"—he or she needs to assume a disciplinary posture at times.

There is a common expression, "turn that frown upside down" (i.e., "turn that frown into a smile"). Chassidut teaches (although not in these colloquial terms), that the smile that comes after a frown is of an even higher level. This is because it not only comes sequentially after the frown, but it elevates the frown itself into a revealed smile.

The modern belief is that "it takes more muscles to frown than to smile" and therefore a smile is always better. Indeed, it is much more difficult for a parent or teacher to say "no" or exhibit sternness, than it is to smile and act kindly. But we learn from the way God conducts the world that, while it may take extra "muscles" or effort to hold back a smile, if children never learn that they have failed, then it is questionable whether they can ever understand what success is, and that it takes effort to get there.

Why is effort so important? Because people with a fixed mindset believe that, for those who are intelligent, success should come easily, so they are embarrassed to work hard. Their perspective is that the need to expend effort gives the impression that they are not so smart after all. By contrast, growth mindset individuals realize that even the greatest natural gifts can be improved.[10] They want to grow, and they realize that effort is the key to continued success in life.

There is a saying from the Talmud,[11] "[If one says] 'I have made an effort but have not found [i.e., succeeded]'—do not believe him. [If one says] 'I have not made an effort and have found'—do not believe him. [But if one says] 'I have made an effort and found'—believe him!" Only those who make the effort will succeed.

A fixed-mindset individual thinks that success depends on innate, predetermined talents. But the growth mindset knows that success depends on hard work. If you work hard, you'll be successful. If you don't work hard, you won't be successful. If you worked hard and weren't successful, don't believe that you worked hard enough. Your success testifies to the effort you put in. This is called working with one's own strength.[12]

And that brings us back to the frown—or, put another way, to constructive criticism.

If you have to be right all the time, that's a fixed mindset. Better to willingly accept criticism, than to ignore or reject it. But if you have a growth mindset, you not only learn from criticism, but welcome it as the Chassidic aphorism states, "Cherish criticism for it will place you on true heights."[13]

SUCCESS OF OTHERS

...feel threatened
by the success
of others

...find lessons and
inspiration in the
success of others

We have now arrived at the last item in Dweck's diagram—reacting to the success of others.

Growth mindset people know what it took to get there, and they admire, applaud and are inspired by those who succeed through genuine effort. But fixed mindset people become irritated or intimidated by the success of others.

The latter is called envy, but the former—even if there is an element of envy in it—is never negative. Indeed, the Talmudic sages say that envy which inspires growth is good: "Envy among scholars augments wisdom."[14] A positive form of envy can spur on effort. And thus we see that, while fixed mindset people arrive at their optimal level of performance in their youth and plateau afterwards, growth mindset people continue to reach higher and, consequently, they strive to achieve and learn more no matter their age.

2

THE KABBALISTIC VIEW

The Behaviorist Model

A great deal of modern psychology is concerned with the observable and measurable side of human behavior, and as such, it tends to dismiss or ignore the spiritual side. Although Dr. Dweck's work bridges several disciplines (including developmental, social and personality psychology) and focuses on human motivation, she is probably unaware to what extent her growth and fixed mindset model mirrors the Kabbalistic model of the behavioral powers of the soul.

Nevertheless, she has contributed to the spiritual nomenclature. She has not only given us new names—"growth and fixed mindsets"—for the good and evil inclinations (the *yetzer tov* and *yetzer hara*), she has also given us new terminology for some of the channels (*sefirot*—סְפִירוֹת) with which God created the world and which permeate all existence, specifically those of the *sefirot* that comprise the lower part of the Kabbalistic Tree of Life:

keter—כֶּתֶר

"crown"

binah—בִּינָה   *chochmah*—חָכְמָה

"understanding"   "wisdom"

da'at—דַּעַת

"knowledge"

gevurah—גְבוּרָה   *chesed*—חֶסֶד

"might"   "loving-kindness"

tiferet—תִּפְאֶרֶת

"beauty"

hod—הוֹד   *netzach*—נֶצַח

"acknowledgment"   "victory"

yesod—יְסוֹד

"foundation"

malchut—מַלְכוּת

"kingdom"

We will shortly see that:

- "challenges" on her diagram correspond to *netzach* (נֶצַח) which is generally translated as "victory" but which also refers to the attributes of "eternity" and "endurance"

- "obstacles" correspond to *hod* (הוֹד) or "acknowledgment" and "thanksgiving"

- "effort and energy" correspond to *yesod* (יְסוֹד) or "foundation" which relates to the power of procreation[1]

- "success of others" on her diagram—which refers to seeing other people's success in a positive light and accepting criticism, and which is shorthand for the rectification of the ego— corresponds to *malchut* (מַלְכוּת) or "kingdom," also translated as "leadership," "dignity," or "nobility."

But before we examine these in detail, it is first necessary to explain some of the pertinent aspects of the *sefirot* in general.

Sefirot: Modes of Divine Influx

Probably the best-known Hebrew word that Kabbalah is responsible for introducing to non-Hebrew speakers is *sefirah* or its plural form *sefirot*.

This is because the most fundamental model used in Kabbalah is that of the ten *sefirot*.

In Hebrew, the meanings of a word can best be understood by first finding the word's three-letter root and then studying the various nouns or verbs that share this same root. The three-letter root of the word *sefirah* (סְפִירָה) is *samech-peh-resh* (ס-פ-ר) and it appears in three different categories of words giving it three distinct meanings—as a brilliant light, as the written word and as a mystical number. Therefore, *sefirah* takes on these three meanings as well:

- *Sefirah* shares is root with "sapphire" (*sapir*— סַפִּיר), whose brilliance is associated with the heavenly throne envisioned by the prophets.[2]

- *Sefirah* also shares its root with "story" (*sipur*— סִפּוּר) and "book" (*sefer*—סֵפֶר), and as such denotes a specific attribute through which God expresses Himself in the world. In this sense God is like an author of a book who expresses himself through the narrative he writes.

- And, finally *sefirah* shares its root with "number" (*mispar*—מִסְפָּר) which alludes to its role in the abstract underlying mathematical structure of creation.

Because of its varied meanings, special attention must be paid to the word *sefirah*. Even though in

Kabbalah, *sefirah* always designates a Divine emanation, nonetheless, its meaning fluctuates with the context in which it is being used.

In general, the three major contextual usages of the ten *sefirot* are:

(1) the ten manifestations of God,

(2) the ten powers or faculties of the soul, and

(3) the ten structural forces of nature.

In Chassidic literature, these three contexts are considered the three basic dimensions of reality and are called Divinity, Souls, and Worlds.[3] When speaking of the manner in which God's self-expression is perceived, the ten *sefirot* are understood as ten manifestations of Divinity. When reflecting on how Divinity is projected into the living experience of a human being, the *sefirot* become manifest as the ten powers of the soul. Finally, we find that the *sefirot* are also cast as the basic structural forces that form our external reality, for example the components of our bodies.

Meaning of the Sefirot	Dimension of Reality	Content
Manifestations of God	Divinity	Manner in which God's self-expression is perceived
Powers of the Soul	Souls	Reflection of how Divinity is projected into the living experience of the human being
Structural Forces of Nature	Worlds	Basic structural forces that form our external reality

It should be stated clearly from the outset that the Almighty, as He exists unto Himself, cannot be understood or even spoken about using any kind of human thought or language. Instead, man can meet God only through the prism of created reality.[4] Through that prism, God appears to us in the form and manner that He chooses.[5]

The ultimate intention or desire for God creating the universe was to make for Himself a "dwelling place" below in the lower realms[6]—including the lowest and most material world of all, the world that we inhabit. Keeping this in mind, as we begin to examine how each item of Dweck's diagram corresponds to the lower *sefirot*, we will not only explain the soul or psyche component, but we will delve into how each concept, while rooted in the spiritual realms, directly guides the material realms, including specific systems within our physical bodies. As we will see, although it may take our intellect some time to adopt to the growth mindset, our bodies naturally act this way from birth.

3

CHALLENGES AND OBSTACLES

Behavioral *Sefirot* in the Soul

Challenges and obstacles complement one another just like *netzach* ("victory") and *hod* ("acknowledgment") which are considered "two halves of the same body."[1] Not to collapse in defeat when confronted by a challenge requires from us the quality of victory or perseverance/endurance, whereas the strength needed to continually overcome obstacles exercises our trait of acknowledgment or thanksgiving.

Netzach (נֶצַח) is the first of the three behavioral *sefirot* in the soul. Its Hebrew root *nun-tzadik-chet* (נ-צ-ח) links it with words that share the same root, including "eternity" (*nitzchiyut*—נִצְחִיּת), and "orchestration" (*nitzuach*—נִצּוּחַ). The implied concept conveyed by words formed from this root is a sense of initiative and persistence which are necessary to overcome opposition. While "victory" assumes that being victorious comes as a result of taking initiative, "eternity" implies persistence/endurance, and "orchestration" presupposes a creative plan that employs both these qualities. As with a conductor in an orchestra, in an educational environment each teacher should conduct the classroom first to foster student participation. Then once the students are engaged, the instruction or curriculum (i.e., the "orchestration") can be presented in a more systemized fashion.

Hod (הוֹד) is the companion soul power to *netzach*, and it expresses itself through two fundamentally-linked forces in creation.[2] The first, and the one we will now address, is intimated by the root of *hod* — *hei-vov-daled* (ה־ו־ד) which appears in the words for "praise/thanksgiving" (*hodayah* — הוֹדָיָה), "acknowledgement" (*hodaah* — הוֹדָאָה) and "confession" (*viduyi* — וִדּוּי). All these meanings represent the capacity to acknowledge a Supreme Power or Higher Intelligence exerting authority over oneself.[3]

Note that this *sefirah* of *hod* suggests a distanced posture of acknowledgment, which allows us to maintain a focused perspective regarding our Divine destiny, as hinted in the verse from the Book of Jeremiah: "From afar God becomes apparent to me."[4] In this sense, the force of acknowledgement can be thought of as internal radar guiding one towards an unseen destination by amplifying the "echo" (*hed*— הֵד from the same root as *hod*—הוֹד) that it produces in the soul.

Given the above, one lesson we can learn is that challenges are active, whereas obstacles are passive. According to Dweck's research, a fixed mindset avoids challenges while a growth mindset embraces them. In either case, implicit is the need to make a firm decision one way or another. When confronted with a challenge, even inaction is active. Take the example of a student during a difficult exam. The test has been placed before him, and he now has thirty minutes to complete it. Whether he decides to persevere through the difficult questions or sit there chewing gum is entirely up to him.

Another lesson is that obstacles are experienced more passively by the fixed mindset because obstacles involve avoidance. Two paths diverge in a forest—one has readily observable hurdles while the second looks free and clear. Even if the first will get one to the desired destination faster, the fixed mindset will still go along the path that looks easier.

In the vernacular, this is called "coasting through life." Like a ship captain planning which course to take, the "coaster" looks for the seemingly easy way out. But unlike the captain, who appropriately has the safety of the crew in mind, the "coaster" is looking for the easy ride through life.

Surfing the Waves

There is a very good allegory—that of surfing—which depicts this interplay between *netzach* and *hod*, or challenges and obstacles, quite vividly. But before we ride the waves, let's first expand our thinking by way of inter-inclusion.

A common example of inter-inclusion is a crystal. When a crystal is cut in half, each half still reflects the whole because every piece of a crystal is representative of every other piece. So, similarly, if you were to "take a piece" of holiness in order to analyze it, you would be taking every aspect of the whole. This applies to the essence of the soul also, as the Ba'al Shem Tov said: "When you grasp a part of an essence, you grasp its entirety."[5]

When we speak of the *sefirot* of *netzach* and *hod*, we can expand these two into four by the simple process of inter-inclusion or two-squared (2^2) like this:

- *netzach* included within *netzach* (נֶצַח שֶׁבְּנֶצַח) "victory within victory"

- *hod* included within *netzach* (הוֹד שֶׁבְּנֶצַח) "acknowledgement within victory" (whereby *netzach* or victory is dominant)

- *netzach* included within *hod* (נֶצַח שֶׁבַּהוֹד) "victory within acknowledgement" (whereby *hod* or acknowledgment is dominant)

- *hod* included within *hod* (הוֹד שֶׁבַּהוֹד), "acknowledgement within acknowledgement"

We explained previously that the willingness to take on challenges characterizes *netzach*, whereas the sense to acknowledge obstacles reflects the more distanced posture of *hod*. In order to explain these two fundamentally-linked forces in creation, Kabbalists refer to *netzach* as masculine relative to the feminine *hod*. It is for this reason that the inter-inclusion of *netzach* and *hod* favors the more active property of *netzach*. Similar to the sages' statement, "It is the man's way to go in search of a woman but it is not a woman's way to go in search of a man,"[6] when explaining the relationship between *netzach* and *hod*, we view *netzach* as the *sefirah* which "goes out" to unite with *hod*. While the two extremes indicate either all male or all female behavior, the two intermediate levels serve to unite the male property of *netzach* with feminine *hod*.

With this in mind we can now understand why the first intermediate stage is female within male (*hod* within *netzach*), and the second male within female (*netzach* within *hod*). A clear explanation of *hod* within *netzach* is that the male principle of self-confidence has an element of female sincerity inter-included within it, whereas *netzach* within *hod* suggests that the female has a male side inter-included within her.

Given our expanded model of four, where would we place the abovementioned example of a student chewing bubble gum instead of concentrating on his difficult test questions?

Sometimes it's hard to detect the difference between challenges and obstacles. But the bubble-gum chewer relates to his test as an obstacle to be avoided not a challenge to be overcome. Therefore, he exemplifies *hod* (passivity) within *netzach* (activity). Activity is dominant here because the student is actively sitting down in the classroom and chewing gum. If he didn't attend school at all that day, then we would say that he is either totally passive (*hod* within *hod*) or at least that his passivity is dominant (*netzach* within *hod*). A student who doesn't plan to take the test later, or maybe has given up hope of passing the course or graduating, has most definitely convinced himself that he is of a fixed mindset. The role of a concerned educator is to bring a sense of "victory" (activity or growth) back to this student through caring and encouraging words. As in the words of Rabbi Yosef Yitzchak Schneersohn, the sixth Rebbe of Chabad, "There is never a lost case."[7]

The ability to see obstacles as challenges to be confronted and overcome relates to the dominancy of *sefirah* of *netzach*, while recognition of the obstacles themselves indicates the dominancy of *hod*. A Chassidic aphorism, which relates to this interplay between *netzach* and *hod*, states: "You can't always go on an iron bridge." That is, you don't always have the opportunity to confront challenges from a firm or comfortable place. The definition of this world is that it is a world of challenges and trials.[8] And to overcome obstacles, you must be willing to travel along "shaky bridges" if you are to achieve your desired objectives.

While many of us do not seek out shaky bridges, there is one type of "shaky bridge" that people not only seek out but, it seems, the "shakier the bridge" the more it is valued. As mentioned, the allegory that we would like to use in this section—according to our four inter-included levels of *netzach* and *hod* — has to do with the art of surfing.

We say the "art of surfing" because learning how to ride the waves or scale obstacles not only takes practice and perseverance, but presents itself as an art form. It not only takes hours of training to know when to "take-off" on the crest of a new wave, "drop" from the crest of the wave to the pit, or "lull" about until the next rideable wave comes along, the results are also picturesque. Let's now see how the different surfing techniques correspond to the four levels mentioned previously:

Victory within Victory

Growth always relates to the *sefirah* of *netzach*. But, along with the ability to win, to be victorious, to succeed at this level, there comes the awareness that all power comes from God. When we decide to take on a challenge, to never give up, it should be with a keen awareness of the Higher Power orchestrating all of creation.

The lesson of *netzach* within *netzach* is never to give up — and this, indeed, is the meaning of victory. Even if we fall, we have to get up again and win. This desire to be a winner, to pick oneself up and try again is expressed well in the epic moment of the "wipeout." When a surfer falls off the surfboard and gets pummeled by the wave, it reminds him how powerless he really is. But, from this discouraging moment, comes the potential for the greatest heights—to recover one's surfboard, pick it up, and go back to the waves for another round.

In addition, to the assertion of Rabbi Yosef Yitzchak Schneersohn that "there is never a lost case"—or in the context of our discussion, "there is no one who experiences a wipeout who can't get up again"— there is the statement of Rebbe Nachman of Breslov: "I have been victorious and I will be victorious."[9] Expressed in this statement is the inter-inclusion of *netzach* within *netzach*, or victory included within victory. To reinforce the relationship between victory and Rebbe Nachman: the numerical value of his Hebrew letters which combine to form the name "Nachman" (נַחְמָן) equals the very word "victory" (נֵצַח)!

Acknowledgement within Victory

The second level relates to those people who are fixed in their passive acknowledgement, but who realize that all of their power to emerge victorious comes from Above. While those with this mindset don't jump over obstacles, they work to remove them. For example, confronted by unjust laws, people using *hod* within *netzach* will actively take on the challenge of reforming them.

It is important for those with an acknowledgment perspective not to overextend themselves just as the surfer who needs to keep the limits of his expertise in mind even while performing the most remarkable stunts. The surfer who tries to impress the crowd too much is likely to end with a wipeout.

The fourth leader of Chabad, Rabbi Shmuel of Lubavitch, encouraged his followers to jump over obstacles in his well-known saying: "The world says, 'If you can't crawl under an obstacle, try to climb over,' but I say, 'At the outset, jump over!'"[10]

At first glance, this seems to be advice to those at the level of *netzach* within *netzach* — to always emerge victorious. But as noted earlier, those at that level do not look at the obstacles for they are busy embracing challenges. Therefore, this statement is directed to those at the level of *hod* within *netzach* who see the obstacle in the way: "Don't stand there and ponder. Jump!" When they do so, they are transformed. Although they initially hesitate in the face of adversity, with the encouragement of Rabbi Shmuel and a healthy dose of inspiration from Above, they can transform their fixed mindset into a growth mindset.

A surfer who has mastered the art of transforming his once fixed tendencies into even greater levels of accomplishment becomes the most prized success story of the surfing tournament. So, too, the most exceptional cases of growth mindsets are those who transformed their previously fixed mindsets.

Unlike the surfer who only takes victory into account—and as a result takes chances and bends the rules and, therefore, may experience wipeouts time and again—the surfer who has learned to include *hod* within *netzach* performs the most amazing stunts without compromising the rules of the discipline.

As for Torah scholars who embrace a *hod*-within-*netzach* state of consciousness, they might be encouraged to learn that the inner dimension of the Torah will help them appreciate even the smallest particle of Torah. As soon as a student enters Rabbi Shimon bar Yochai's mystical world, the analytical limits on the Torah are broken and the examination and understanding of much smaller phenomena begins.

Normally, when we think of numerical values in the Torah, we think of counting the number of verses or words. One of the differences between the revealed and concealed teachings of the Torah is that the revealed teachings do not in general go beyond the level of meaning related to a single word. In other words, the analytical strength of the revealed tradition of interpreting the Torah stops at the level of a word. But, the concealed tradition resolves the Torah even further, delving into letters, and smaller and smaller quanta of the text.

A result of the additional resolving power of the inner dimension of the Torah is that there is a greater sensitivity to the fact that the smallest of the small counts just as much as the biggest of the big. This is also a lesson that the expert surfers have learned. If an expert surfer really wants to impress the crowd with his greatest feats and win tournaments in the most spectacular ways, the greater his understanding of the finer details of the discipline, the greater the chance that very "big" outcomes will occur. But, as just explained, the greatest feat is the "surfing" that is done through the inner dimension of the Torah.

Victory within Acknowledgement

Although this level is a step down from the "winner" mentality of previous two levels, this does not mean that the obstacle will never be overcome. But as in our bubble gum chewer example, passing the test may take some time. The fact that the student continues to attend class is already a sign of potential growth. What remains to be seen is whether his willingness to show up will translate into a mastery of the material, or at least the ability to get a passing grade come report card time.

In surfing terminology, this level relates to the surfer who shows up each day to learn and practice but doesn't necessarily tackle a wave. He acknowledges that there is a learning curve to become an expert surfer, so at the very least, he makes his trek to the beach to learn by watching and observing others.

According to Kabbalah, *netzach* corresponds to the right leg whereas *hod* corresponds to the left. Similar to the predisposition of a surfer to experience a wipeout, both the right and left legs are always on the verge of falling down. So, more than any other *sefirot*, the *sefirot* of *netzach* and *hod* require the most encouragement. As Rebbe Nachman of Breslov, the *tzadik* who most typifies victory, also stated, "There is altogether nothing to despair about."[11]

Interestingly, while we are usually encouraged to choose the right over the left—as in the teaching from the Talmud, that if one arrives at a crossroads and is unsure what to do, one should turn to the right[12]—a surfer is called a "goofy foot" if he rides with his right foot forward on the board. This concept is expressed well in *netzach* within *hod*. While both the right and the left foot are needed, the left of *hod* is considered the dominant or preferred foot of the two in that particular combination, even though it is relatively passive compared to the right of *netzach*.

Acknowledgement within Acknowledgement

This last level corresponds to one of the most celebrated days of the Jewish calendar, *Lag Ba'Omer*—the anniversary of the passing of the author of the *Zohar*, Rabbi Shimon bar Yochai. *Lag Ba'Omer* (the 33rd day of the Counting of the Omer period) is known as the day of the giving of the inner dimension of the Torah, also called Kabbalah, for it was the day on which Rabbi Shimon revealed the deepest mystical secrets of Judaism.

During the 49-day Omer count—which occurs between the holidays of Passover and Shavuot—each week corresponds to one of the seven lower *sefirot* and each day corresponds to each of these *sefirot* included within one of the other seven. In this way, we arrive at 49 inter-included *sefirah* combinations. The day when Rabbi Shimon passed away, the 33rd day, is the fifth day of the fifth week, which corresponds to *hod* within *hod*, or "acknowledgement within acknowledgement."

The power to reveal the inner dimension of the Torah that we experience on that day stays with us the entire year. Rabbi Shimon himself teaches that "through this book (the *Zohar*), we will go out of exile with compassion."[13] At this level we also don't back off from obstacles but, rather than jumping over them, sneak under them or proceed past them in a natural way.[14]

Returning to our surfer metaphor, it is clear that *hod* or "passive acknowledgement" for a surfer relates to the surfing time spent riding the hollow "barrel" or "tube" of the wave. When the wave comes over the surfer's head and covers him, he can still prevent a wipeout by comfortably riding the hollow of the wave. Although this approach is not as active as surfing atop the crest of the wave, the surfer is still considered to be overcoming the obstacle of the wave even if he assumes the passive mode of *hod*.

We can also apply this metaphor to the two ways in which we approach Torah learning itself: While the revealed or legalistic dimension of the Torah is surfed from the outside on the "crest of the wave," the inner dimension of the Torah or Kabbalah is surfed from the inside on "the inner hollow of the wave."[15]

The intention a surfer should have while riding in the hollow of the wave is the experience of the inner dimension of the Torah, or the "Divine Nothingness" that precedes any genuine flash of insight. To be sure, even though it appears that riding atop the wave is of utmost importance, in some ways riding the inner hollow or tunnel can be even more so. The letters that comprise the Hebrew word for "wave" *gal* (גַל) are the same as *Lag* (ל״ג) and are both equal to 33. So in addition to reminding us about the inner dimension of the Torah, riding the tunnel of the wave can also remind us of *Lag Ba'Omer*, or the day when the Torah's inner dimension was given.

The Downside

While we've been speaking in the positive about *netzach* and *hod*, there is a negative counterpart to these four levels as well. Sometimes a growth mindset can be negative, as is the case in the willingness to accept a challenge because of a feeling of personal strength. As noted earlier, the proper perspective comes with the realization that all strength comes from Above.

These two *sefirot* of *netzach* and *hod* are not only inter-related, but balanced like the measuring pans on a scale. Although we should always remember that God is the source of all strength, we should also never think that our efforts have accomplished nothing. Both matter and both are necessary for success.

Long Short Way

We mentioned earlier that the terms "fixed mindset" and "growth mindset" correspond to "evil inclination" and "good inclination" respectively. Since we are trying to reframe the topic of mindsets using classic Jewish terminology, we will now introduce a metaphor from the sages called the "long short way."

> Rabbi Yehoshua ben Chananiah said: "Once a child got the better of me. I was traveling, and I met a child sitting at the crossroads. I asked him, 'which way to the city?' and he answered: 'This way is short and long, and this way is long and short.'
>
> "I took the 'short and long' way. I soon reached the city but found myself obstructed by gardens and orchards. So I retraced my steps back to the crossroads and asked the child: 'My son, did you not tell me that this is the short way?'
>
> "Answered the child: 'Did I not tell you that it is also long?'"[16]

The author of the *Tanya*, Rabbi Schneur Zalman of Liadi bases his entire exposition of Divine service on the moral behind this story from the Talmud, as is apparent from the opening page of his book, where he states:

[This book is] based on the verse, "for [the Torah and its precepts] is something that is very close to you, in your mouth, in your heart, that you may do it" [17] — to explain, with the help of God, how it is indeed exceedingly close, in a long and short way.

Although a discussion of the history behind the *Tanya* is beyond the scope of this book, suffice it to say that the *Tanya* was meant as a written manual for navigating the psyche. Its author writes: "[Here] one will find tranquility for his psyche, and true counsel on everything that he finds difficult in the service of God."[18]

As we will see, the best way to understand the metaphor of the "long short way" is through psychology. Being as the first fifty-three chapters of the *Tanya* are essentially therapy sessions in writing, it must be that the allegory that starts it all somehow relates to something fundamental in the psyche. As there are thousands of allegories to choose from in the Talmud and beyond, why did Rabbi Schneur Zalman choose this particular one?

Rabbi Schneur Zalman expected his followers to first study, comprehend and meditate upon the essential truths of existence. Only after they had invested immense effort to grasp and relate to these truths on the intellectual plane of the soul could they hope to reach the emotions of the heart.

This approach relates to the *sefirah* of *netzach*, to victory and perseverance in the soul, and—on the practical level—to the willingness to accept challenges, the domain of the growth mindset. Just as most wars are not won in a day, it takes persistent effort to keep on moving forward even if the road ahead seems long and arduous.

While it may seem easier to cleave to God with heartfelt love, Rabbi Schneur Zalman's intellectual approach begins with the mind. He maintains that only once we have correctly oriented our mind, can we truly connect to God by means of the properly directed emotions of our heart. This is the "long short" route that eventually leads us to our destination.

Some may argue with this regimen and demand a more direct path. This mindset (which we now call the "fixed mindset") sees only obstacles in the way, and feels disheartened at ever achieving the goal of true connection with God. People who possess the fixed mindset don't mind studying and following the Torah and its commandments, but like the readers of thousands of self-help books on the market, they expect that the results be immediate. They want to see the finish line from the starting point. This approach is referred to as a "short long way."

The reason why a book like the 2006 best-seller, *The Secret*—which claims that positive thinking can bring about life-changing results such as increased health, wealth and happiness—has sold close to 20 million copies is probably because the publisher's marketing department did such a good job promoting the "short long way." But even those books which, unlike *The Secret*, are based on solid research instead of pseudo-mysticism are missing the point if they don't convey the importance of long-term perseverance. Even worse than books that lead the reader nowhere are those that lead the reader down the wrong path altogether.

While society today seems to favor the seemingly short, easy way to success, this is not the advisable path to take. The "long short" way is much harder to market, with its winding and tedious steps. But these initial "setbacks" and frustrations set a person on a higher path. Because the "long short way" demands every ounce of intellectual and emotional stamina, the person on this road is continuously tested to achieve more. Notwithstanding the initial difficulties, this is the road that leads—steadily and surely—to the desired destination.

Clearly, Dr. Dweck's approach, based on decades of research is much better than *The Secret*. In addition, she tries her best to sell her version of the "long short way." This is no easy task, as there are thousands of other pop-psychology or self-help books out there that will tell the reader the opposite. Nevertheless, she states her case, and has been successful at having it accepted as well.

She explains the importance of effort and perseverance as follows:

> As children, we were given a choice between the talented but erratic hare and the plodding but steady tortoise. The lesson is supposed to be that slow and steady wins the race. But really, did any of us ever want to be the tortoise?
>
> No, we just wanted to be a less foolish hare. We wanted to be swift as the wind and a bit more strategic—say, not taking quite so many snoozes before the finish line. After all, everyone knows you have to show up in order to win.
>
> The story of the tortoise and the hare, in trying to put forward the power of effort, gave effort a bad name. It reinforced the image that effort is for the plodders and suggested that in rare instances, when talented people dropped the ball, the plodder could sneak through.[19]

In the coming pages, we are going to speak more about growth, praise and effort. But the important thing to keep in mind now is that sometimes parents or teachers try too hard to protect their children or students from life's difficulties. But instead of steering them away from the turbulence or hurdles along the path, they should instead try to condition their charges to view each apparent setback as a springboard to eventual success. Although adults, with their extra years of experience, see the winding path ahead, nevertheless they should still be willing to teach optimism and resolve in face of it.

Challenges and Obstacles in the Body

We should not leave the subject of challenges and obstacles without mentioning how the body deals with them in the physical sense.

Netzach corresponds to the endocrine system, comprising glands and hormones, while *hod* corresponds to the immune system. Of all the systems in the body, these are the two most recently understood in the medical world to function together. So, too, as noted earlier, *netzach* and *hod* function together.[20] In the words of Kabbalah, these two are "two halves of the same body,"[21] or colloquially, "two sides of the same coin."

The endocrine system is the body's ability to take on challenges that stand in the way of its growth and development, that is, those processes that ensure sound health and longevity. Working to generate new cells and structures within the body, the hormones of the endocrine system perpetuate the life of the body and aid it in overcoming the obstacles of time.

Netzach is also understood in Kabbalah as the "milk" that nurtures the growth and development motivated by the *sefirah* of "loving-kindness" (*chesed*—חֶסֶד), from which it branches out on the right axis in the Tree of Life model of the *sefirot*.[22]

The inner experience which motivates *netzach* is "confidence" (*bitachon*—בִּטָחוֹן). Rectified self-confidence is ever conscious that God always stands at our side to give us the power to succeed in our self-initiated endeavors.[23] In order to grow and develop spiritually, a child must be taught[24] to acquire a balanced, rectified sense of self-confidence.[25] Indeed, rectified self-confidence must be nurtured in a child's consciousness just as an infant nurses on its mother's milk.

An imbalance in hormones may reflect an imbalance in the inner sense of confidence. In order for the hormone system to properly regulate the body's metabolism, we must learn how to manifest and regulate, control and orchestrate our energies. (As we mentioned earlier, one of the meanings of *netzach* is "orchestration.")

The *sefirah* of *hod* corresponds to the immune system, the physiological system that fights disease. The immune system monitors what properly belongs in the body and what is a foreign invader. A healthy immune system annihilates destructive foreign intrusions into the body, while an unhealthy immune system turns against the body itself.

As mentioned earlier, the *sefirah* of *hod* also relates to "thanksgiving," and its inner power is sincerity. Sincerity implies honesty in all our social transactions. To strengthen the immune system, we must cultivate in our soul a sense of thanks to all those who have been kind to us and acknowledge our indebtedness to others, both for their physical as well as spiritual gifts to us.[26] With sincere acknowledgement of our indebtedness to others, transcending egocentric subjectivity, we reach the objectivity necessary to recognize an ally or a foe, to link to the ally and fight off the foe, both on the spiritual and physical planes.

4

EFFORT

Foundation in the Soul

Our discussion of the "long short way" metaphor introduced these dueling dynamics between challenges and obstacles, or *netzach* and *hod*, in the soul.

As mentioned in the initial analysis of Dr. Dweck's diagram, effort is fundamental because it reorients a person towards something purposeful. Instead of viewing the world as a place of entitlements, those who value effort—the growth mindset—appreciate the toil that goes into accomplishments. Whereas those with a fixed mindset, having taken the "short long way," never do reach their destination. On the other hand, those with a growth mindset persevere step-after-step toward the finish line following the "long short way."

In Kabbalah, effort corresponds to the rectification of sexuality,[1] or the *sefirah* of "foundation" (*yesod*—יְסֹוד). *Yesod* is repeatedly referred to in mystical sources as the force of "totality" or "all" (*kol*—כֹּל), insofar as it is the repository for all the energy from the *sefirot* that precede it, as well as the channel for directing that energy into creation.

The verification of selfhood or self-realization is the very essence of *yesod*. Whereas *netzach* and *hod* represent the promise of self-fulfillment, *yesod* brings that promise to fruition. Together, the three properties of the soul we have explained thus far— *netzach*, *hod* and *yesod*—take the soul from an abstract reflective position, to one impelled towards concrete and active involvement within the real world. *Yesod* is where the months or years of intellectual and emotional preparation are eventually realized.

A *tzadik*—identified in the Torah with *yesod* or "foundation"[2]—is a righteous person who is always ready to exert maximal effort in order to achieve an end. (This idea is similar to the statement of the Talmud quoted above regarding toil and effort.[3]) Each of us possesses the potential to be a *tzadik* if, like the *tzadik*, we apply effort to realize our mission in life.

The more effort we exert at the foundation level, the more we will see our potentials realized. This requires both constant involvement, and exertion to the greatest degree possible, for *yesod* is "all," as noted. If we immerse ourselves totally in the task at hand, then we can begin maximizing the potential latent in the *sefirah* of *yesod*.

The epitome of effort is self-sacrifice, totally giving ourselves over to accomplish a goal. In previous generations, self-sacrifice included the literal sacrifice of life in order to sanctify the Name of God. But, in our generation, what is expected is the complete absence of self-gratification, even from the good things we do. To accomplish a goal, we need to be willing to fall before the finish line, in order that the person behind us can see the correct way to the end.

For the sake of procreation, a parent has to be ready for self-sacrifice. This would mean accepting the possibility that the parent may never reach the finish line. This was the case with King David, who throughout his life aspired to and planned to build the Holy Temple in Jerusalem. Although he himself didn't reach his goal, his son King Solomon did. King David's self-sacrifice for the cause of building the Temple was realized in his son, even though he wanted to complete the task himself. So, too, this awareness that procreation may lead the parent to have children who will outpace his or her own ambitions and efforts in life is a good example of absence of self-gratification, even from good things.[4]

Those whose soul-root is centered in *netzach* should also be aware of the Chassidic adage that self-sacrifice can lead one to "jump off the roof," but not to "jump on the roof." Meaning that while *netzach*— or the rightist approach to life—is prone to overextending itself, a right mindset with proper attitude toward self-sacrifice (*hod* within *netzach*) knows that there is no sense in trying to "jump onto roofs." Over-extending oneself to self-sacrifice in vain doesn't do anyone any good and can just be a wasting of energies. In an extreme state this could lead to a mental breakdown, whereby one feels the need to continuously sacrifice more and more.

The *netzach*-centered people are often prone to feel too much pride or self-confidence in their own actions, without fully recognizing that everything comes from God. On the other hand, the *hod*-centered people are prone to back off from obstacles and never to take initiative. Either extreme leads to what Kabbalah calls the "breaking of the vessels," or a disconnected sense of self (or selflessness) that leads one to be either too confident or too defeatist, acknowledging reality as it is but not trying to impact or change anything.

One Who Serves, and One Who Serves Not

In our previous discussion, we moved along the diagram from the first two levels of challenges and obstacles, to the third level of effort. As we introduced the first two levels with an allegory from the *Tanya*, it is appropriate that we should bring an additional allegory to better ingrain in our minds what effort should mean to us. As the *Tanya* is a manual written to heal the psyche, it is fitting that this allegory be also one of the *Tanya*'s best-known teachings.

The way Rabbi Scheur Zalman explains effort is by contrasting a person who "serves God" and one who "serves Him not." He first quotes the following verse from the Book of Malachi: "And you will return and see the difference between the just man and the evil one, between he who serves God and he who serves Him not."[5] And then he goes on to explain how the sages interpreted this verse:

> This explains the Talmudic statement[6] that "he who serves God" refers to one who reviews his studies one-hundred-and-one times, while "he

who serves Him not" refers to a person who repeats his lesson no more than one hundred times. This is because in those days it was customary to review each lesson one hundred times. The Talmud illustrates this by an example taken from the marketplace, where donkey-drivers used to hire themselves out at a rate of one *zuz* (Talmudic-era silver coin) for ten *parsi* (Persian miles), but for eleven *parsi*, they charged two *zuzim* because driving the eleventh mile exceeded their customary practice.

Therefore, this one-hundred and first revision, which is beyond the normal practice to which the student had been accustomed since childhood, is considered equivalent to all the previous one-hundred times put together.

In fact, its quality surpassed them in endurance and effort, hence entitling him to be called "he who serves God."[7]

What makes us strong is our willingness to continuously wage the war against our evil inclination. And this is the ultimate goal that a growth mindset individual should strive for. Notwithstanding any fixed tendencies, the growth-oriented person manages to persevere amidst challenges and overcome obstacles. Rabbi Schneur

Zalman explains that "he who serves God," is written in the present tense, for it describes a person who is still laboring hard in his Divine service.

King Solomon says in the Book of Proverbs: "For a *tzadik* falls seven times and rises, but the wicked shall stumble upon evil." [8]

It doesn't take much to dissuade people from exerting effort when they are stuck in the past, or willing to yield to their evil inclination. But a *tzadik* exerts maximal effort time and again, never distracted from the holy task at hand. In our discussion, the *tzadik* relates to the growth mindset, while the evil one relates to the fixed mindset.

To view yourself incapable of change and of not having the ability to emerge victorious over your evil inclination is not just an injustice that you do to yourself alone, but to those others who could have benefited from your good actions. Remembering this should be of help, as well as remembering that God never sends you a test that is too difficult to overcome.

The Body's Way to Express Effort

The *sefirah* of *yesod* manifests itself in the physical plane as the reproductive system, the innate capacity to re-produce or re-create oneself in the form of progeny.

The inner experience of *yesod* is truth or verification, in the sense of self-realization or self-fulfillment. Clearly, there is no greater self-fulfillment than physical reproduction,[9] bringing into the world another soul, who is a reflection of the self created in the image of God.[10]

To strengthen our reproductive system, we must make every effort to realize our life's dreams. This is the power of the soul of Joseph, the archetypal soul of *yesod* in Kabbalah, who saw his dreams come true.

In modern society, we often make the mistake in thinking that pursuing a career in order to fulfill ourselves in life contradicts devoting ourselves to marriage and raising a family. In truth, self-fulfillment in all avenues of life and devotion to raising a family are interdependent. Self-fulfillment begins with the conscious realization that the greatest possible self-fulfillment is reproduction and raising a family—fulfilling the blessing that God gave man on the day of his creation: "Be fruitful and multiply and fill the earth and conquer it..."[11]—and this does not prevent us from simultaneously pursuing a career, contrary to what others may think.

Indeed, one of the cautionary messages that Dr. Dweck brings is not to be concerned about what others think about us. If we act in order to further our self-image (or in the case of students, reputation amongst our classmates), we are playing into the trap of the fixed mindset:

> [The perception is that] either you have ability *or* you expend effort. And this is part of the fixed mindset. Effort is for those who don't have the ability. People with the fixed mindset tell us, "If you have to work at something, you must not be good at it." They add, "Things come easily to people who are true geniuses."
>
> ...People with the growth mindset, however, believe something very different. For them, even geniuses have to work hard for their achievements. And what's so heroic, they would say, about having a gift? They may appreciate endowment, but they admire effort, for no matter what your ability is, effort is what ignites and turns it into accomplishment.[12]

This brings us to our next section. If we should emphasize effort over appearance, then in order to appreciate this in greater detail, we need to better understand what appearance is.

5

APPEARANCE

Revealing the Light Within

Before we proceed to the analysis of the next two stages in Dr. Dweck's mindsets diagram—accepting criticism and relating to the success of others—we first need to introduce an intermediary level between effort and criticism as it is understood by Kabbalah. Between *yesod* (which we have equated with effort) and *malchut* (which we have equated with accepting criticism and relating to the success of others) is a stage called "the crown of foundation" (*ateret hayesod*—עֲטֶרֶת הַיְסוֹד). While Dweck alludes to this stage many times in her book, she doesn't explicitly identify it as a level unto itself. But as we are basing our analysis on the Kabbalah, we decided to make this slight emendation to her diagram.

The first thing to keep in mind is that *ateret hayesod* issues from *yesod* to become the source of *malchut*, the *sefirah* immediately below it. While it actually stems from *yesod*, it is an additional property of the soul and corresponds to an additional physiological system—the skin.

Skin defines appearance. In a feminine context, it is praiseworthy that a wife beautify herself for her husband and be well-kempt in every respect. In the masculine context, appearance translates into the desire to appear successful in accordance with the world's estimations—such as feeling the need to pursue a career instead of raising a family. In this sense, appearance reflects a fixed mindset.

In the masculine context, the Jewish male is subject to the ritual of circumcision which is a process performed on the skin of the male reproductive organ. This process involves the removal of the thick foreskin and then the peeling back of the thin mucous membrane to reveal the crown of the organ. In this way, the initially coarse physical skin is refined and made capable of reflecting spiritual light.[1] Hence, the "covenant of circumcision," (*brit milah*—בְּרִית מִילָה)—specifically, the manifestation of the "crown of the organ," also called *ateret hayesod* (עֲטֶרֶת הַיְסוֹד)—corresponds to the physiological system of the skin throughout the body.[2]

Now let us examine the feminine aspect of this spiritual dynamic.

As we will subsequently explain at length, the feminine *sefirah* of *malchut*, receives energies from the six emotive *sefirot* above it. As in the physical realm, the culminating union in the spiritual realms is also between the relatively masculine foundation (*yesod*) and the feminine kingdom (*malchut*)—*yesod* is represented in the physical by the male procreative organ that gives life, while *malchut* is that which receives it and completes it.

Whereas *ateret hayesod*, or the male procreative organ, refers to the relative state of *malchut* within *yesod* (the concluding ability of *yesod* to populate *malchut*), from the feminine perspective it is the reverse. The fertile feminine womb represents the collective soul of Israel, or in the terminology of Kabbalah, *yesod* within *malchut* (the ability of *malchut* to nurture the physical or spiritual seeds which are left from the union with *yesod*). In the female, the womb is the rectified receptive power of the soul that guards itself from foreign invasion and fights off enemies, while sanctifying itself to receive and nurture the seed given to it from above. Once the womb is ready to receive, the light-filled seed of the crown of the covenant[3] can impregnate the feminine to bring a new life into the world. Spiritually, this relates to the power of the Jewish people to become a "light unto the nations,"[4] and achieve lasting peace between the lamb (themselves) and the wolf (the nations of the world).[5]

Whereas the mindset of the male—at this level of *ateret hayesod*—is to complete the rectification of *yesod* by bringing down new Divine light into the world, the work of the female is to properly nurture this new light. As a result, the feminine behavioral response is to ensure that the world is a fitting receptacle to receive this new light in purity. She needs to be protected from foreign invasion, from elements that would profane her innate purity. As explained at length in our book *Body, Mind, and Soul*,[6] this translates in the psyche as overcoming the fear of rape (one of the three primal fears of the human psyche—the other two being fear of insanity and fear of murder). This primal fear is represented in the Biblical account of the rape of the concubine of Gibeah.[7]

In Kabbalah, Benjamin corresponds to the womb, the physical location that experiences the fear of being raped by the "wolves" of the world. In the positive sense, however, the soul-root of Benjamin represents the power within every Jew to prepare the world to be a fitting receptacle for new Divine light.

As noted, while the feminine is concerned with both receiving the light and nurturing it, the masculine is primarily concerned with bringing the light down. In practical terms, this means that if any new theory is to be proven correct, both its masculine and feminine components must be proven to be successful—that is, both the (masculine) innovations in thought and the (feminine) real-world consequences. If, as a result of the theory's propositions, people are led to live better, more fulfilled lives, then this is a sign that the new influx of ideas has found a home in the world. But the concern that the theory will be misused, misrepresented, or not used at all, are all questions that the feminine mindset raises. As the feminine seeks to sweeten or heal reality, her concern is that these "drops of light" should "give birth" in the real world.

For the Sake of a Drop

A story adapted from the writings of the sixth Lubavitcher Rebbe, Rabbi Yosef Yitzchak Schneersohn, illustrates this well:

Rabbi Pinchas of Koretz was among the most distinguished disciples of the 18th century founder of the Chassidic Movement, the Baal Shem Tov; he was also a close companion of the Baal Shem Tov's successor, the Maggid of Mezeritch. Rabbi Pinchas was of the opinion that the holy teachings of Chassidism should be safeguarded. He believed that these esoteric ideas should not be publicized, but shared only with a select few. He particularly opposed those who transcribed the Maggid's teachings and actively distributed copies to the wider Jewish community.

Once, while Rabbi Pinchas was in Mezeritch, he found one such transcription languishing in a mound of garbage. The sight of this caused him great pain. Rabbi Schneur Zalman of Liadi, the founder of the Chabad Movement, was also in Mezeritch at the time. Wishing to assuage Rabbi Pinchas' feelings, he began to speak in metaphor:

> Once upon a time, there was a mighty king who had an only son. In his youth, the son, the heir to the throne, fell gravely ill. The doctors were unable to find a cure for his illness. A call was issued throughout the land, offering great reward for the one who provided the cure. But all the great doctors, all the famed scholars, were silent, for they knew no remedy for the illness of the prince.

Then there arrived a man who knew of a proven remedy for the illness of the prince. He described a certain precious stone which—if ground to the finest of powders, mixed with superb wine, and given to the prince to drink— would cure him.

This gem, however, was extremely rare, and could not be obtained anywhere in the kingdom and beyond. The only specimen in existence was at the centerpiece of the royal crown of the king. Removing this gem would mean destroying the crown—the king's most precious possession and the ultimate symbol of his sovereignty.

At first, the king's ministers were overjoyed to discover the gem. But as soon as they realized that by removing the stone from the crown—the very one with which their king was crowned— his glory would fade, they were extremely distressed. Nonetheless, they were forced to inform the king that the gem had been found.

The king was overjoyed. He commanded that the gem be extracted and ground to a fine powder, and that the potion for his son be quickly prepared.

But, before this could be done, the king was suddenly informed of terrible news. The prince's condition had deteriorated—so ill was the prince that he could take nothing, not even liquids, into his mouth. The experts and scholars assembled at the palace were certain that, under the circumstances, the king would surely direct that the stone not be ground, so that the splendor of the royal crown could be preserved.

How astounded they were to hear the king instructing them to hurry and crush the gem and to prepare the potion as swiftly as possible, and to pour it into the mouth of the prince. "Grind, pour, squander the entire gemstone," said the king. "Who knows? Perhaps a single drop will enter the mouth of my son, and he will be healed!"[8]

This is what the feminine mindset says—that all is well worth the effort as long as at least one drop brings light and healing to the world.

Psychological Implications

Now that we have explained some of the underlying principles behind the new level that we added to Dr.

Dweck's mindsets diagram, we can discuss the psychological implications.

Whereas the soul-root of Benjamin represents the power within every Jew to prepare the world to be a fitting receptacle for new Divine light, the soul-root of Benjamin's older brother, Joseph, represents the ability to bring more of this light down into the world. These two directions are called "arousal from above" (Joseph), and "arousal from below" (Benjamin); while the masculine direction is to bring down new light from above, the feminine approach is to take this spiritually low world and elevate it.[9]

Although in this model Benjamin corresponds to the feminine, in another model Benjamin corresponds to the masculine—indeed, he represents the "wolf." However, in every abiding and growing relationship, there must be these two opposite yet complimentary natures; thus, relative to Joseph, Benjamin is considered feminine. These roles need not be absolute. For instance, in a study session between close friends, each one takes a turn reading and discussing the subject matter, while the other listens. To be in an attentive or listening frame of mind is a relatively receptive or feminine characteristic when compared to the one who is conveying new information. Also, for instance in a

Torah class, the students "absorb" the light of the teachings presented by their teacher, at least until the question-and-answer session that follows the teacher's lecture; then they may offer their own insights. This is the nature of any giving/receiving relationship. For the connections to grow stronger, there needs to be both give and take.

In relation to the growth mindset, only a teacher with a growth mindset knows how to effectively accept a listening posture during the class discussion. Rabbi Chanina makes a strong statement on this subject in the Talmud: "I have learned much from my teachers, more from my colleagues, and the most from my students."[10]

In modern society, being able to listen is usually a quality associated with politeness. But from the Talmud we learn that the greatest growth teachers can attain is to learn how to properly become students of their students. This Talmudic statement should remind even the most knowledgeable teachers how to stay on the path of growth.

The Joseph Archetype

Earlier, when we introduced the *sefirah* of *yesod*, we said that it manifests itself as the reproductive system, and that to strengthen our reproductive system, we must make every effort to realize our life's dreams, which is the power of the soul of Joseph, the archetypal soul of *yesod* in Kabbalah.

The Torah relates that Joseph, while a slave in Egypt, withstood the test of sexual temptation, resisting the inappropriate advances of his master's wife:

> Joseph grew to be well built and handsome. In the course of time, his master's wife cast her eyes on Joseph, "Sleep with me," she said. He adamantly refused ... She spoke to Joseph every day, but he would not pay attention to her. He would not even lie next to her or spend time with her. One such day, he came to the house to do his work. None of the household staff was inside. She grabbed him by his cloak. "Sleep with me," she pleaded. He ran away from her leaving his cloak in her hand, and fled outside.[11]

Joseph's repeated and forceful resistance of the considerable pressure Potiphar's wife brought to bear rectified his "covenant of circumcision," *brit milah* (בְּרִית מִילָה) on the deepest possible level.[12] For this reason, he is called "Joseph the Righteous" (*Yosef HaTzadik*—יוֹסֵף הַצַּדִּיק).

It is important to remember that Joseph was only seventeen at the time, which suggests that this intermediate level of "appearance" very much relates to youth, especially to the tests of sexual temptation that young adults go through in their adolescent years.

The Torah repeatedly refers to Joseph's good looks,[13] but to better appreciate why—and what this tells us about the concept of "appearance"—we need to go all the way back to Adam and Eve.

Before God vanquished Adam and Eve from the Garden of Eden, the Torah states that He made them "tunics of skin."[14] The Talmud notes that in the Torah scroll of the Mishnaic Sage, Rabbi Meir, it read "tunics of light." When the *brit milah* is pure and rectified, it glows and all one's skin begins to radiate, as was the case with Adam and Eve prior to the primordial sin.[15] Instead of the opaque ectodermal tissue of today, their skin was light-filled and electric.

This helps us better understand what this level of *ateret hayesod* means for us. While physiologically, it relates to skin, spiritually, it is the source of the light that we shine outwardly to others. If we see a man shining with light-filled holiness, then most probably this comes in the merit of his guarding the purity of *ateret hayesod*. And this is what people saw about Joseph.

When Joseph was thrown into prison after Potiphar's wife accused him of rape, the Torah states:

And God was with Joseph, and He showed him kindness, making him find favor with the warden of the prison. Soon the warden had placed all the prisoners in the dungeon under Joseph's charge. He [Joseph] took care of everything that had to be done. The warden did not have to look after anything that was in his care. God was with [Joseph] and God granted him success in everything that he did.[16]

The ability to attract people and invite success like a magnet comes in the merit of the light of the skin, or a holy, handsome appearance. According to Kabbalah, the law of attraction begins with the rectification and safeguarding of the covenant of circumcision, the *brit milah*.

The first person to undergo circumcision in the Torah, the Patriarch Abraham, was promised fame and fortune. Abraham, who taught the world to believe in one God and attracted all of mankind to follow in his path of loving-kindness, became the father of many nations. To him, God promised:

"I will make you into a great nation, I will bless you and make your name great, and you will be a blessing. I will bless those who bless you, and curse those who curse you, and through you, will be blessed all the families of the earth."[17]

Holy, Handsome Appearance

There are no shortcuts to this state of being—and a holy, handsome appearance does not come easily. It is not the same as beautifying oneself with cosmetics or excessively focusing on externalities. This especially applies to men.

Whereas, in Jewish law, women are encouraged to beautify themselves for their husbands, to look in mirrors and make the most of their appearance, men should not.[18] Men and women are likened to the sun and the moon. The sun shines its direct light to the moon, and the moon reflects this light. So, too, for a male who has worked on himself to guard his covenant, the purity of his *brit milah* and the essential light of his procreative seed is solely for his wife. The external light that emanates from his skin—in the form of fame or glory—is for the sake of inspiring others, not for his own aggrandizement. Just to appear impressive or macho is an external or secular version of all that we have now discussed, a negative quality associated with the fixed mindset.

Dr. Dweck often mentions in her book that this sort of externality, the need to impress, fosters a fixed mindset. Fixed mindset people may never acknowledge that they need to work hard in order to succeed. Instead, they try to present to the world that they are a natural genius, wealthy, and so forth—all of which is very much a reflection of their self-image. In relation to appearing "righteous," they want to seem like the perfect *tzadik*, without having to overcome the temptations of "Potiphar's wife" (which, unfortunately, one does not need to look hard for to find today in modern society).

While not using this terminology, Dweck implies that she also views "appearance" as an intermediary stage between exerting effort and accepting criticism. She notes that those focused on external appearances are, in general, closed to accepting any form of criticism or appreciating the hard-earned success of others. As she puts it:

> We now know that there is a mindset in which people are enmeshed in the idea of their own talent and specialness. When things go wrong, they lose their focus and their ability, putting everything they want…in jeopardy.[19]

> Fixed-mindset leaders, like fixed-mindset people in general, live in a world where some people are superior and some are inferior. They must repeatedly affirm that they are superior, and the company is simply a platform for this.[20]

Speaking specifically of women, Dweck notes that women have a special problem in this regard because they are ultra-sensitive to the opinions of others.

> This vulnerability afflicts many of the most able, high-achieving females. Why should this be? When they're little, these girls are often so perfect and they delight in everyone's telling them so. They're so well-behaved, they're so cute, they're so helpful, and they're so precocious. Girls learn to trust people's estimates of them. "Gee, everyone's so nice to me; if they criticize me, it must be true." Even females at the top universities in the country say that other people's opinions are a good way to know their abilities.[21]

The fact that women are more sensitive to the opinions of others about themselves than are men reflects once more the origin of feminine psychology in *ateret hayesod*, which we have identified with self-awareness and appearance. Ideally, women should try to reach a proper balance between their innate feminine receptivity to what others think and say about them, and the masculine approach which, when corrected, does not put such strong emphasis on external appearance and the opinions of others.

6

CRITICISM AND THE SUCCESS OF OTHERS

Evil and Holy Kingdoms

Finally, we arrive at the last two stages in Dr. Dweck's diagram which, for growth mindset are: being able to accept criticism, and relating positively to the success of others. In our Kabbalistic model, these two levels relate to the *sefirah* of *malchut*.

Malchut can be understood as positive or negative. Whereas the "evil kingdom" (*malchut haresha'ah*— מַלְכוּת הָרְשָׁעָה) lacks a sense of lowliness and is therefore unable to accept criticism, the "holy kingdom" (*malchut dikdushah*—מַלְכוּת דִּקְדֻשָּׁה) possesses an existential sense of lowliness and therefore willingly accepts criticism.[1] If you see a king or leader who is full of arrogance and unable to accept criticism, these are clear indications that his kingdom is from the "other side" (i.e., not from the side of holiness).

For a king of a holy kingdom is humble. Indeed, the archetypal figure of the holy kingdom is King David, who most exemplified the property of lowliness. He said to his wife Michal, "and I shall ever be lowly in my own eyes."[2]

The *sefirah* of *malchut* is close to the level of *ateret hayesod* or "crown of the covenant" which is immediately above it. In fact, as we mentioned previously, these two levels unite. Accepting criticism and relating positively to the success of others is the feminine version of its masculine counterpart, that of a rectified state of appearance. Those who have not rectified their state of appearance try to promote their self-image to the world. They are not willing to accept criticism nor are they able to relate positively to the success of others. But those leaders with an inner sense of lowliness will be able to lead their "kingdoms" without feeling the need to impose oppressive dominance on their "subjects."

The outward appearance and rule of a true king should be naturally felt by his subjects without the need for totalitarian behavior. King David teaches us to lead by being lowly in our self-estimation. If we see ourselves as "custodians" in relation to the task at hand—instead of recipients worthy of honor and majesty—we can then begin to fulfill our purpose in the world. The same holds true for responding to the success of others. If we feel threatened by another's accomplishment, then this is also because of ego. The objective should be to emulate King David and lead humbly, while also learning from everyone we meet.[3]

Kingdom in the Soul

The role of *malchut* is to rectify creation by providing the ground for creative energies to bear fruit. While the union between husband (*yesod*) and wife (*malchut*) results in physical children, there are many more implications to this union. Consistent with them all—whether physical or spiritual seeds are sown—is the intent that the result should help build a more perfect world. Once a new seed/drop reaches earth, as with our story of the king's son, then this is an indication that both the masculine and feminine energies in the union have become manifest—both the conveyance of new, light-filled teachings and the realization that even a drop from these teachings can heal at least one person down here in our world.

Being willing to receive is only one of the two primary dynamics at play in *malchut*. The "higher order," as it were, is God's enforcement of His program for creation itself. While God wants to influence and pervade the material realm with the light of Divine consciousness, He also wants the material realm to be readily submissive to this influx.

It is the posture of receptivity or existential "lowliness" (shiflut—שִׁפְלוּת) that expresses the inner essence of kingdom. Indeed, God—the King over all creation—lowered Himself, so to speak, onto the throne of glory from which He directly oversees His creation. While this seems counter-intuitive, it is the property of lowliness that allows us to act with "kingly" responsibility toward the created realm. One who is a true king realizes that the only reason he was initially granted power and responsibilities was in order to use it to perfect God's reality.[4]

Properly-directed lowliness guarantees that our actions in life will be motivated by the highest standards. Like King David, only when we become "lowly" in our self-estimation, can we begin to actualize our purpose in life.

What we have begun to appreciate is that lowliness goes a long way towards assisting a growth mindset. Although some might think that a lowly person is sluggish and unmotivated, in fact, the opposite is the case! Only by derailing from the train of personal aggrandizement, can we honestly assess ourselves and our place in the world and begin moving forward. Although King David ruled over hundreds of thousands of subjects, he still didn't lose sight of his own existential lowliness.

Although this may come as a surprise, it is through embracing lowliness that we receive the strongest impetus to succeed. For instance, if we give all the credit to God for the good that we do then, in addition to the actual acknowledgement, we also prevent ourselves from "getting in the way" of the good that we do. When we allow ourselves to become enamored by our own actions, we fall into the trap of the fixed mindset. While flattery only leads to an inflated sense of ego, the self-awareness that characterizes the *tzadik* leads to the opposite. As mentioned before, by not feeling self-satisfied with his accomplishments and investing added effort, the *tzadik* continuously experiences the full potential of the present in every moment of the day.

The greatest obstacle to achieving or reaching a growth mindset is the credit we take for our accomplishments. An author with a proper sense of lowliness realizes that like a cursor on the screen, he is not the one writing the book. Even if the book later sells millions and he becomes famous, he still does not take credit for it. He knows that the only reason why he was given credit rather than someone else is because God decided to choose his "cursor" that day. This is how David viewed his kingship.[5]

Digestive System

In order to better appreciate what it means to be lowly and internalize light, let us again turn to a physiological system of the body. Because the final *sefirah* of *malchut* relates to the ability to digest necessary components from the outside world and extract the "sparks" of nourishment, it is explained that *malchut* corresponds in the body to the digestive system.[6]

Whether the nourishing sparks come from the mineral, vegetable or animal kingdoms, when they are ingested, they become transformed into vital human energy. Digestion operates as a clarification process whereby useful elements from the environment are assimilated into the body, while waste products are expelled.[7] *Malchut* involves the elevation into the body of "fallen sparks" of energy that are extracted from the products of the earth below.[8]

The process of elevating fallen sparks requires the property of lowliness. In order to find, identify and redeem the sparks of Godliness in the levels of creation beneath us, we first need to begin by lowering ourselves to each respective level—whether it be mineral, vegetable, animal.

Then, when expelling waste products from the body, we should meditate on our own state of existential lowliness. This is also true on the spiritual plane, whereby a healthy digestive system depends upon a sense of lowliness, the power to lower ourselves to that which is below us, and the longing to return to God with our cache of fallen sparks.

Digesting Criticism: A Story

This is the story of how a rabbi of a European community learned to digest criticism and give credit where it is due—to God.

> He had been a community rabbi for thirty years, when he fell out of favor with the communal board, and they decided to look for a replacement. Since you don't unseat a rabbi, they left him formally in his previous position, while simultaneously hiring someone else. Everyone started going to the new rabbi, and the old rabbi who had given thirty years of his life to his community remained heartbroken. He felt like everything that he had acquired over his life had been taken away from him. He was

already in his 60s and was becoming more and
more physically ill from what had transpired.
Finally, when his situation became most severe,
someone told him that he should meet Rabbi
Asher Freund in Jerusalem. Feeling as though
he had reached the end of what he could bear,
he travelled to Jerusalem and came to Rabbi
Freund.

Rabbi Freund met with him, and the rabbi
started telling him what happened—that not
only did the community do him an injustice by
bringing in someone new (when really there
was nothing wrong with him), but that on top
of it, the new rabbi they had brought to replace
him was no good for them, because of x, y, and
z.

As he was listing his reasons, Rabbi Freund
suddenly stopped him and sternly reproached
him: "How dare you! You come to me telling
me about the needs of your community, about
how much they need a good rabbi, how this
new rabbi is not this nor that. But the only thing
that you care about is yourself. The only thing
that you care about is what you did, and you
want payment for it, you want everybody to
recognize and honor you. But you have to

understand that God is telling you 'No, you've done enough! God took it away from you because all that you're interested in is yourself!'"

And so he talked to him very harshly for several minutes until this former rabbi broke down in tears. He came back to Rabbi Freund the next day, and Rabbi Freund said that he had already told him everything there was to say— he was no longer the rabbi of his community, and that was it. He should go back home and live out the rest of his life, being thankful for all that he had received.

This man flew back and really took to heart what Rabbi Freund had said to him. He realized that, in fact, he was only concerned about himself. He began to see that he had rationalized his hurt feelings, and convinced himself that his younger replacement didn't know enough. He couldn't accept the fact that he was rejected. He couldn't take it because his self-image wouldn't allow him to. He—the important and successful spiritual leader—was being ousted and replaced.

After a month of working on himself, he came to the point where he began thanking God for the many good years he had enjoyed as the rabbi of the community. He had been given the wonderful opportunity to do what he loved, to serve and help others in spiritual matters. He suddenly realized that all those years of being busy with the needs of the community were a gift from God, a pure and simple gift that he did not deserve for any particular reason. God gave him the opportunity to be so busy over these years, and now it was over. It was all a gift, and he now realized that just as he had not earned the gift, he had nothing to complain about when God decided to take it away.

Rabbi Freund had told him to take himself, his ego, out of the picture. And this he proceeded to do. He realized that he was not the center around which everything else revolves. So what can he claim to have accomplished over these past thirty years? For himself, nothing. All his success as a communal leader was not his to begin with. It was God's. God had given him the privilege of doing all the good things that he had done. He had no reason to take credit for his achievements. If God had so desired, He could have given the opportunity to someone else. The man started thanking God for the great gift that He had given him, and after a few more weeks, he came to the point of feeling joyful again. He decided to spend the rest of his life learning Torah.

A week after he had settled into a new routine, involving learning and prayer, the new rabbi who the community had been brought-in to replace him suddenly disappeared. The communal board decided that they had made a mistake and pleaded with the old rabbi to return to his previous duties. And so, he returned to being the community rabbi. But, now, having realized what a tremendous gift he had been given (twice), he did not let an hour pass by without thanking the Almighty for the opportunity to do what he so loved.

The moral to be gleaned from this story is that failure was an essential part of the picture when viewed in its entirety. God really didn't want the rabbi to stop leading his community. He was indeed the right person for the job! He was meant to continue, just in a different way. Before, he had viewed all his communal activities as revolving around himself, but God gave him the opportunity to change his point of reference. In the end, God actually gave him the greatest gift—the gift of understanding that all of his deeds were not his; they all belonged to God.

Two Levels of Kingdom

When discussing the *sefirah* of *malchut* in relation to Dr. Dweck's mindsets diagram, we identified it as corresponding to both "accepting criticism" and "relating positively to the success of others." Now, we are ready to address how each of these represents a unique level within *malchut*.

The first and highest level is *malchut* in its source Above, before it descends to the lower worlds. The second is *malchut* after it descends and begins to influence the particulars of this world. To explain via metaphor:

A king rules over his subjects in two ways: He is removed from his subjects and only "sees them" from a distance. While this has advantages—in that rich and poor appear equal—this is still considered "ruling from afar." Although he is king, the subjects do not feel that he has a personal interest in their lives and well-being. But then there comes a time when the king "descends from his throne" in order to rule more directly and then he interacts much more closely with his subjects.

As we mentioned previously, the king's "descent from the throne," or *malchut*'s descent into this world, reflects a posture of receptivity or existential lowliness that serves as the inner essence of this *sefirah*. Although we said previously that God lowered Himself, as it were, onto the throne of glory, there are times when God descends from His throne and lowers Himself even further, in order to show His individual care and concern for each and every one of His subjects. This is aptly illustrated by Rabbi Schneur Zalman of Liadi in his explanation of the difference between the months of Elul (the month which precedes Rosh Hashanah) and Tishrei (the month of Rosh Hashanah and Yom Kippur), which also explains the difference between these two levels of *malchut*.[9]

Rabbi Shneur Zalman explains that in Elul, when we repent and attempt to cleanse ourselves of sin, God is up close and personal. He is likened to a king who leaves his inner sanctum of the palace and goes out into the field, where all His subjects can meet him. Meeting God in Elul—out in the field—is an informal encounter, in which we seek His fatherly kingship over us on a personal level. However, once we enter the month of Tishrei, which begins with Rosh Hashanah, we are keenly aware that God has again ascended his throne of judgment, and we again feel His mighty presence in His palace.

The month of Elul—with its focus on self-examination and repentance—relates to "accepting criticism" whereby we are ready and willing to listen to the constructive words of rebuke or advice that may otherwise be hard to hear. Important to remember is that the ability to listen comes from feeling close to the one who is giving the advice. We are more willing to accept criticism when it comes from someone viewed as a fatherly or motherly figure.

It should be noted, however, that whereas feeling close to God is more openly manifest in Elul, throughout the year God rules over every particular of creation. Even during Rosh Hashanah and the month of Tishrei, a time known for the relative distance of rule, there is still a judgment on every detail of creation by means of Divine Providence.

The Torah account of Jacob's behavior at the well is an example of how rebuke should be given. When Jacob arrived at the well, he saw three flocks of sheep with their shepherds resting beside them though it was still early in the day. He asked them, "My brothers, where are you from?"[10] and then he engaged them in some small-talk before he told them, "The day is yet long; it is not the time to gather in the livestock. Water the sheep and go pasture."[11]

The 11th century Torah commentator, Rashi, explains that Jacob saw the shepherds lounging around by the well instead of pasturing their flocks, and he rebuked them for not having done an honest day's work. But before he offered his rebuke, he first addressed them as "my brothers" and inquired about their origins. Only then did he speak to them more pointedly.[12]

This also relates to the month of Elul. Since God wants us to repair and amend our past misdeeds, He first comes to us in the field with mercy, compassion and a smiling countenance, and only then withdraws back to His palace for the commencement of the judgment of Rosh Hashanah in Tishrei.

In the Torah portion usually read during the Ten Days of Repentance between Rosh Hashanah and Yom Kippur—*Parshat Ha'azinu*—Moses' rebuke of the Israelites is clearly motivated by his love for his people, and his words are coated with sweetness to those with a sensitive ear. As the *Tanya* explains, love that can be expressed only within the outwardly harsh context of a rebuke is actually a higher level of love than that which can be expressed openly.[13]

Recognizing the Success of Others

This brings us to the subject of false rebuke which is not motivated by love but by jealousy.

Harsh words result when we sense that the gifts that were given to others came from Above, but we are not willing to admit it. However, the true "golden path" to success begins when we acknowledge that everything comes from God. Only then can we ourselves become truly successful.

If we think that we deserve something and it doesn't come our way, we are apt to get upset when our expectations are not met. But the more we realize that *everything* that we have is a gift from God, the more we will be able to accept and relate positively to the success of others.[14]

Chassidic literature derives the correct approach to success from *Ethics of the Fathers* teaching that it is better to "be a tail of lions rather than the head of foxes."[15]

In Kabbalah, the fear of the lion relates to the fear of murder. This is the fear that at first prevents a person from going outside, to the "field" (as in our Elul metaphor), in order to redeem the sparks of holiness held captive during the period of exile.[16] This is made clear by the Book of Proverbs, which states,

"The lazy man says, there is a lion outside! I will be murdered in the street!"[17]

As noted, Elul is a time to return to God in repentance. The recognition in Elul is truly that it is better to "be a tail of lions rather than the head of foxes," meaning that it is better to be a subject to the King of kings than an important and cunning person who others look up to (the "head of foxes").[18]

The month of Tishrei, however, is the time to coronate the "head" of the King. This is accomplished by proclaiming and renewing our commitment to God's kingship over all of creation, beginning with Rosh Hashanah, the "head of the (new) year." This includes the willingness to go "outside" of our house and comfort zone in order to fulfill the commandments of the King with great intensity and vigor.

The month of Elul—in keeping with the "tail of the lion"—is a time to exhibit our existential lowliness as subjects of the King of kings. And the joyfulness of being the "tail" relates once more to the ability to accept criticism. This is the time when we are most ready to listen to constructive criticism from those we care about.

But Tishrei, when God ascends His throne and rules from afar, is a time to equalize the poor and wealthy alike before His majesty. Tishrei is the month when we are most willing to accept the success of others, because it is when we are most aware that success comes from Above.

Like gold itself, success that comes as a result of inborn talents and abilities is given as a gift from Above to each specific soul according to its role and purpose in life. The important thing is not to dwell on the gold of others, but to uncover the gold within oneself. While the purpose of physical gold will only be revealed in the future with the construction of the Third Temple, we can begin to contribute our "bar of gold" to the building today by acknowledging that all success comes from Above.

In summary:

Challenges, Obstacles, Effort, Appearance, Criticism and Success of Others in the Soul and Body

Level on the Mindsets Diagram	Sefirah	Psyche	Physiological Systems
Challenges	Victory (netzach—נֶצַח)	One who rises to accept challenges	The Endocrine System
Obstacles	Acknowledgement (hod—הוֹד)	One who has the strength required to continually overcome obstacles	The Immune System
Effort	Foundation (yesod—יְסוֹד)	One who grows through effort	The Reproductive System
Appearance	The Crown of the Reproductive Organ (ateret hayesod—עֲטֶרֶת הַיְסוֹד)	One who has the desire to shine new light to the world	The Integumentary (Skin) System
Accepting Criticism	Kingdom (malchut—מַלְכוּת)	One who is lowly enough to receive criticism	The Digestive System
Relating to the Success of Others		One who is willing to learn from everyone	

7

THE JEWISH APPROACH TO GROWTH

The Question of Praise

At the beginning of this book, we questioned whether it is wise to praise others at all. If our motivation is to foster a growth mindset (especially in children), maybe we should forgo praise altogether and simply encourage everyone to keep improving themselves.

Dr. Dweck deals with the question of praise in the parent-child setting. One negative example that she offers is praising a child who did well on a test by saying: "Wow. You're really smart!" This type of praise, she says, will create in him a fixed mindset. But, if praising a child in this way is not good, then how should a teacher or parent inspire good grades?

Dr. Dweck explains that the difference between acceptable praise and praise that should be avoided is in *what* is praised. If you praise the effort rather than the success, then you are on your way to nurturing a growth mindset in the student. She suggests praising good grades by saying, "You did really well, so you must have worked hard—you must have put a lot of effort into studying." By praising the child in this way, she says you are introducing the correlation between "effort" and "success." The good grade (in this instance) should be correlated more as a product of effort, instead of a subconscious trigger that establishes reliance on natural-born intelligence.

While Jewish tradition also weighs effort heavily, there is another important nuance in the way that a Jewish educator or parent should approach praise. In addition to emphasizing the effort, clear reference must also be made with regard to the end result of the effort. For instance, instead of just praising the effort needed to get a good grade, it is better to say; "It's nice you got a good grade on the test. You must have worked hard, and it shows that you really must understand the material now!"

This approach is helpful for several reasons. The first is that it accounts for those students who get good grades without the effort. The second is that even if the student thought he understood the material, effort turns the superficial knowledge needed to get a good grade into something that will remain with him his entire life. This is especially true with regard to Torah learning, whereby every amount of extra effort takes the student through to deeper layers of understanding.[1]

As is stated in *Ethics of the Fathers* is: "If I am not for myself, who will be for me. But, if I am only for myself (meaning: I trust in what I have been given from birth, my innate qualities), then what am I?"[2]

You have to work hard, regardless of what you have been given. According to the growth mindset, everything depends on toil.

A Third Possibility

As we mentioned, according to Dr. Dweck, there are two ways to praise—either you praise a child for being smart, or for having worked hard. In addition to the added emphasis on results, the Torah approach to mindsets also considers a third possibility beyond praising either native ability or hard work. This we call the praise of prayer.

While we agree with Dweck that a child should be praised for working hard, not for being smart, we have to ask: Where does God fit into the picture? Would it not be best to praise a child as follows: "If you were successful on a test, it must also be that God helped you in your effort; perhaps you prayed hard and He answered you." This is something very important to instill in the life and mindset of a child.

In addition to praising effort, we should also praise the steadfast prayers behind the results. If a student received a good grade on the test because she worked hard, we should also make sure to emphasize that she must have prayed hard as well. While we don't want the student to rely on native intelligence alone, we do want to impress upon her where all success (and everything else) comes from.

At first, the subject of praise seems like a straightforward topic. But in reality, there are a multitude of nuances in praising someone, especially a child. Even if one is speaking the same words, every subtle change in the way the praise is conveyed makes a significant difference to the inner intentions of the heart. Whereas incorrect praise can lead the child down the path of self-aggrandizement, proper praise helps to reframe personal pursuits into Divinely orchestrated undertakings.

More essential than what is actually prayed for is the awareness that true success depends on properly directed prayer. This is why praise at this level includes the addendum: "...you must have prayed hard." Whatever the student wanted to accomplish, it was in the merit of her heartfelt prayer to God that she was successful.

Of course the intention is not that prayer should be viewed as a vehicle to get a good grade on the test, and so forth. A child should be reminded that the best "result" of her prayers are the prayers themselves; the heartfelt connection to God. Thus instead of viewing the results as the goal, a parent or educator should convey that the greatest result of favorable outcomes is the closeness that was fostered between the child and God.

The Balanced Middle Axis

This is the third possibility which balances the two extremes—the growth and fixed mindsets—in keeping with the middle axis of the Kabbalistic Tree of Life. And, in so doing, it includes both the right and left simultaneously. A story about Rabbi Schneur Zalman of Liadi helps explain this idea:

> From the time that Rabbi Schneur Zalman appointed his son, Rabbi Dov Ber to teach young chassidim, Rabbi Dov Ber made very stringent demands upon his students. At the moment they didn't achieve, there was disappointment all around. Then one chassid

asked him: "Do you think that we are all the children of your father [and can achieve your level]?" This statement really moved Rabbi Dov Ber.

Later, Rabbi Schneur Zalman told this young chassid, "Thank you for educating my son…"

This story shows that some things are indeed fixed. Not everyone can be born a son to Rabbi Schneur Zalman, and no matter how hard the chassidim worked, they could never be Rabbi Dov Ber. While the default approach is that we shouldn't look at our lineage or past to determine our future, there are instances where it does make a difference.

The growth mindset is free will, while the fixed mindset is determinism. But, there are certain things that are indeed predetermined, like family heritage or the traits we are born with. So a proper balance is needed between both mindsets.[3] Even though the main point of education should be to teach growth, it must be recognized that the other, fixed side is present as well.

Rebbe Nachman of Breslov also nurtured the growth mindset in his chassidim. He said to them, "You should all try to be like me,"[4] because he didn't want them to be satisfied with doing less. Rebbe Nachman didn't want his followers to say that, since he has a lofty soul and was a descendent of the Ba'al Shem Tov, they might be content with exerting less than maximal effort. He wanted them to try as hard as they could to reach the same level.

At first glance, these two stories seem to be saying the opposite of one another. On the one hand, Rabbi Dov Ber is being told by a chassid that not everyone can be like him, for he has the distinguishing characteristic of having Rabbi Schneur Zalman as his father. No matter how hard a chassid works, he can never become the physical son of Rabbi Schneur Zalman! But Rebbe Nachman is saying, "Don't pay attention to lineage. Be like me anyway."

We learn from these two stories how to reach the perfect balance between the attitude of the growth mindset, together with the recognition of a certain amount of fixed elements, of determinism.

In the first story, the deterministic element was raised only in order to keep the chassidim motivated toward a growth mindset. They had become discouraged by the stringent demands put upon them by Rabbi Dov Ber. In such a case, it is praiseworthy to explain to them that they are not falling short. If a student is feeling that even his best efforts are somehow not up to par, the educator *should* offer words of encouragement so that the student becomes the best that *he* can be. This was so richly illustrated by the famous statement of Rabbi Zushe of Anipol: "When I come to stand before the heavenly court, I do not fear the question: 'Why weren't you Moses?' But I tremble for the day that it will be demanded of me: 'Why weren't you Zushe?'"

But when the chassidim are in high spirits and are ready to listen, then there is no need to place limits on growth. As the Prophet Zachariah says, the nature of a Jew is to be, "a mover among those who are standing."[5] Since Jews are always meant to move or walk, there is truly no limit to growth.

In our generation, Rabbi Menachem Mendel Schneerson, the Lubavitcher Rebbe, also said that his followers should try to be like him. Even though his father was perhaps the greatest Kabbalist of his generation and he was the son-in-law of the previous Rebbe, the truth is that we can still be like him or Rebbe Nachman. But when we doubt our ability to overcome the challenge of becoming a great *tzadik*, then it is good to fall back on the timeless advice of Rabbi Zushe.

Praise in Worlds, Souls and Divinity

Earlier, we introduced a teaching of the Ba'al Shem Tov[6] that in every element of reality there are three dimensions: 1) the outer dimension of Worlds, which is created reality; 2) the inner dimension of Souls, which are the Jewish souls within the Worlds; and 3) the third dimension of pure Divinity, where God is both one and all within creation. We are created with a good and an evil inclination in order to perfect the first two dimensions of reality and to manifest the third.

Now we will relate this concept to praise.

While it is certainly true that we should favor a growth perspective in life, the ability to grow exponentially beyond what we think capable comes from our awareness of God. Because God is infinite, by connecting ourselves with God, we realize more of the infinite capacity within ourselves. While this infinite consciousness should be expressed with utmost humility, once we become connected with the infinity of God, our potentials also seem unlimited. What seems like a world full of deterministic limitations becomes a place full of open-ended potentials.

So again, you can either tell children that they are smart, or you can praise them for the effort they have expended. While the former fosters a more deterministic view of the world (e.g., either you were born as Rabbi Dov Ber, Rebbe Nachman, or not), the latter is truly endless. This second approach is what the Ba'al Shem Tov refers to when he speaks of the level of Souls. The highest way is to praise the Divine influx that people bring to the world through their efforts; and, as God is infinite, so too, the potential inherent at this level is also infinite.

Focusing on a child's native intelligence is praising at the level of Worlds. We tell the child that he succeeded because of the natural talents he was born with. In modern culture, we say that the child has a gift, or some other inborn skill. We may even call him a prodigy, one of the highest accolades today.

The transition from praising someone at the level of Worlds, to the higher level of Souls occurs when we praise effort instead of natural talents and abilities. Souls must be distinguished from angels. Whereas souls are always on the move, angels are relatively static. While souls are defined by their ability to overcome obstacles, we fully expect angels to rely on their innate gifts.[7] This is why we should make sure to praise the "moving" or growth aspects of souls for, as a result of the soul's ability to innovate itself, it merits being called a soul.[8]

This is also at the core of Dweck's theory (though it is not presented by her in these words). But what we are now adding is that when we praise effort, we are praising that aspect of people that makes them souls and not angels to begin with.

The third level is praising children for the Divine input that they have brought down through their efforts and prayers. These efforts may be noticed, or they may go unnoticed. Regardless, praising at the level of Divinity expresses our appreciation for the Divine influx brought down to the world, whether we see the difference or not.

In summary:

Dimension	Praise	Approach
Divinity	Divine Influx	Your efforts bring Divine influx to the world through heartfelt prayer.
Souls	Effort	You can overcome obstacles and succeed.
Worlds	Natural Talent	Either you were born with it or not.

8

FIVE TYPES OF EFFORT

Circular vs. Straight

In order to better explain what it means to either transcend nature through effort, or imbue it with a greater Divine influx, we will use the Kabbalistic concepts of circles and straight lines. These are called *igulim v'yosher* (עִגוּלִים וְיוֹשֶׁר), literally "cycles and straightness." While "cycles/circles" are relatively fixed (because they go round and round), growth moves in a "straighter" way (because it progresses).

The 16th century Kabbalist known as the Ari taught that all of creation has five levels of consciousness. In the soul, the lowest of these five levels of consciousness is called the "psyche" (*nefesh*—נֶפֶשׁ) and relates most closely to the cyclical or fixed mindset.[1] In contrast, the ray of Divine light that God projected into the primordial void, in order fill creation with His light, is called "straight" (*yosher*—

יֹשֶׁר). Unlike curvature, straightness in the soul relates to a more dynamic or growth mindset. It also marks the ascent to the second level of the soul called "spirit" (*ruach*—רוּחַ).

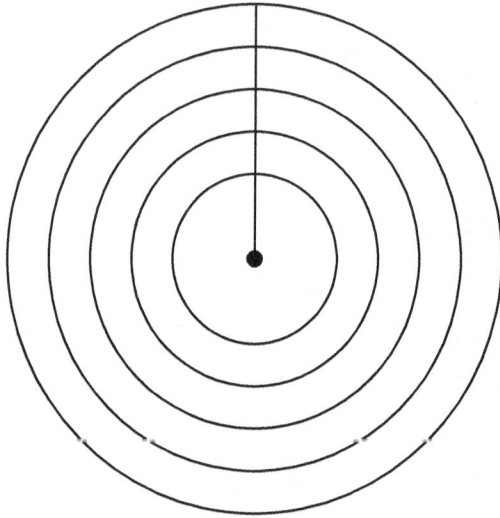

Whereas nature is considered cyclical in Kabbalah, through our efforts we have the ability to make our "second nature" more straight or dynamic. Since roundness is simple—with no clear beginning or end—the circular aspects of our lives can take us either toward holiness or the opposite. But the "straighter" we become, the more we are able to set clear and positive goals for ourselves.

Negative curvature is the fixed mindset of the just-getting-by individual, who contents himself with following the cycles of nature. When it is summer, he goes on vacation; when it is winter he turns on the heat and makes a hot cup of cocoa. But once a person becomes conscious of the infinite God, he comes to recognize that growth or straightness is "hard coded" into every particle of creation itself.

The Hebrew word for "nature" (*teva*—טֶבַע) connotes curvature, as does the word for "ring" (*taba'at*—טַבַּעַת), which comes from the same root. Signet rings were worn by kings and held the royal "seal" (*chotam*—חוֹתָם) atop the ring. Thus the seal introduced the element of straightness into the otherwise round nature of the ring. The ability of a king to stamp and seal his decree for the provinces under his rule relates to the union of the masculine *sefirah* of *yesod* (foundation) and feminine *sefirah* of *malchut* (kingdom).

Important for our discussion is that the effort required to enact a decree makes the world more "straight" or dynamic according to the wishes of the king. Whereas a physical king of flesh and blood does this in order to broaden his rule over his subjects, each person who seeks to live according to the growth mindset also does this to an extent. But, as was explained, the challenge for leaders is not to exert themselves over others in a superficial, domineering or oppressive way.

People can fool themselves to think that their seal or signature should be bigger or more prominent than everyone else's. But unless it comes with a proper sense of lowliness (as exemplified by King David), this assertiveness becomes an expression of arrogance and not the initiative coming from a true leader.

The best seal is the Divine signature of the King of kings, which is stamped on every particle of creation. Through our work to "stamp" more of creation with Divinity, we also make the world a straighter place. As it says, Torah is a path of straightness.[2] If we occupy ourselves only with the cycles of nature, we will "spin our wheels" around the circumference, without ever penetrating the space within the circle.

Positive roundness begins by breaking through these cyclical tendencies. Instead of the predictable motion of a wheel, every bit of effort transforms our path into a forward trajectory, of spiral-like motion, that keeps course on an ascent toward Godliness.

Another word in Hebrew deriving from the same root as "cycle" (agol—עָגֹל) is a "wagon" (agalah—עֲגָלָה) or "circuit" (ma'agal—מַעְגָּל). But whereas wagons relate to the tendency to traverse the circumference of the cycle or the surface layer of the earth, circuits already can take us deeper.[3] One most important reference to the word "circuit" is in Psalm 23, where King David states: "He restores my soul; He leads me in 'circuits of righteousness' for His Name's sake."[4]

Perhaps no figure in the Torah is as closely connected to the growth mindset as King David. In this prayer—that his "circuits" should penetrate and rectify reality—he is also implying that he will not be satisfied with living the life of a "fixed mindset" individual.[5]

Three Missing Levels

The Ari explained that, following the *tzimtzum* (initial contraction of God's infinite light), revealed reality consisted of only these two levels of curvature and straightness. That is, only the two lowest levels of the soul—"psyche" (*nefesh*—נֶפֶשׁ) and "spirit" (*ruach*—רוּחַ)—remained of what existed of God's infinite light before the contraction. What happened to the three higher levels: the "soul" (*neshamah*—נְשָׁמָה), "living spirit" (*chayah*—חַיָּה), and "singular soul" (*yechidah*—יְחִידָה) of reality?

To find them, we need to go into the deeper Chassidic writings that describe the state of things before the initial contraction. The three higher levels, which correspond to the three higher levels of the soul that seemingly disappeared, are known as "primordial" (kadmon—קַדְמוֹן), "one" (echad—אֶחָד), and "singular one" (yachid—יָחִיד).

While we mentioned that effort relates to straightness, in truth there are a total of five categories of effort. The first category—that on the level of "psyche" (nefesh)—is questionably effort, as this is the category that includes the just-getting-by individual who is exerting minimal effort and who is opting out to follow the cycles of nature. But, at each of the four progressive levels, there is definitely effort and straightness being exhibited. Indeed, between each successive level, "quantum leaps" of effort can be observed.

We mentioned previously that a tzadik is known for the continual effort he invests. But while he extends himself beyond his comfort zone, in some ways, his acts are also still perfunctory. When he prays, learns, or does other mitzvot, this is already something that he is relatively used to. His actions in terms of effort can't compare to that required by the ba'al teshuvah (someone who has returned to God and His Torah). In this sense, the innate gifts of the tzadik—those traits and abilities that we usually attribute to the fixed mindset—relate to a degree to the holy actions that he performs. However, a *tzadik* would not be a *tzadik* if he did not invest new energy, and he does so on the second level of "spirit" (*ruach*).

In short, what Dr. Dweck calls the "fixed" and "growth" mindsets, we now call the levels of "psyche" or "spirit" in the soul.

As we live in a post-*tzimtzum* reality, we need to expend more effort to reveal the relatively hidden higher levels of soul. While these three have no correspondence in her theory, the purpose of introducing them now is to show how straight or dynamic our growth can become.

In our search for the three higher levels of effort, which correspond to the three higher levels of the soul—"soul" (*neshamah*), "living spirit" (*chayah*) and "singular soul" (*yechidah*)—we return to the three terms mentioned in some of the most advanced Chassidic writings: "primordial" (*kadmon*), "one" (*echad*) and "singular one" (*yachid*).

Squares, Circles and Curls

In Kabbalah, "primordial" (*kadmon*) relates to the union of a square and circle—more specifically, the square that fits into a circle, or, as we explained before, the square seal within the round signet ring.

To "stamp" present reality with something "primordial" takes a level of effort that is more dynamic than simply pushing oneself to do more. As we said, a *tzadik* is relatively cyclical compared to the *ba'al teshuvah*. The returnee to God and His Torah is the one who most fits "squares into circles," or who infuses more of his previously "circular" or secular life with a new sense of "straightness."[6]

We mentioned earlier that while curvature is a sign of being fixed, as with the fixed mindset, straightness connotes growth. If you are a straight person, you are on the way up. Straightness also oftentimes is synonymous with honesty, as in the verse, "The deeds of the Rock [God] are perfect, for all His ways are just; a faithful God, without iniquity He is righteous and straight."[7]

The straighter or more honest we are, the more dynamic our progress.

In order to become "straighter," we all should emulate the example of the *ba'al teshuvah* and seek to correct our past deeds (and inaction) with even greater effort and fervor. For a *ba'al teshuvah* retroactively transforms his past to reflect a straighter or more honest present, demonstrating that it is more dynamic to fold more circles into an otherwise straight space than continuing on a straight forward trajectory like the *tzadik*. This also applies to a *tzadik* who views himself as someone who is always straightening or fixing his past. However, even then, a *tzadik* progresses at a fixed velocity; whereas a *ba'al teshuvah* accelerates faster and faster.

While the allegory of a king with his royal seal helps us understand this third level of effort to a degree, the visual component may still seem abstract. Another allegory that may shed additional light is one that physicists—specifically string theorists—use to explain why we do not experience more than three spatial dimensions. They say that the additional dimensions are curled up. Here is how they illustrate it:

Imagine a garden hose that is strung out between two buildings. If we look at it from a great distance, it seems like a one-dimensional line. But, from the perspective of an ant walking on the hose, there is of course another circular dimension on which it can walk. Now what happens if the ant decides to walk around the hose? From our perspective, from afar, the ant seems to suddenly disappear; it is as if it went out of existence because we cannot see that the hose has another dimension.

This is the metaphorical way that curled up dimensions are described. But this is a very simple, layman's explanation which addresses only spatial dimensions but not the time dimension.

But now let's think of our garden hose again and try to illustrate the dimension of time and not just of space. What would it mean to have a curled up time dimension? It would mean that there is some inherent cycle that is running around (or inside) the straight or linear coordinate of time.

There is a very basic (but important) lesson we can take from the garden hose example. That, from afar, the *tzadik* and the *ba'al teshuvah* appear to be treading on the same line. Only upon closer inspection will the onlooker realize that, whereas the *tzadik* is traveling on a relatively one-dimensional line, the *ba'al teshuvah* is traveling on a three-dimensional hose comprised of circle after circle. With every step on the "hose," the *ba'al teshuvah* is rectifying a "circular" past into a straighter future.

A Question of Size

The consummate *ba'al teshuvah* in Jewish history — the one who is known for travelling upon circuits, or travelling in a spiral along the length of the hose (so to speak) — is King David. It is also fitting that he referred to himself as a small worm: "I am a worm and not a man; a reproach of man, despised by peoples."[8]

And yet there were times in his life when David was certainly "very big." For example, when he battled Goliath, the giant who had unjustly made himself "big" over the Jewish people. There is such a thing as proper Jewish pride, and David expressed this quality at that time. His desire to fight was not for his own sake, but for that of his people and God. While Goliath mocked the Jews and the God of Israel, David stepped forward in order to show what it means to have a holy sense of "bigness."

This is a good example of how "big" and "small" are relative. Whereas the ant in the garden hose example is viewed as small when seen from afar, we could view a David-like personality as small if we ourselves are far from holiness.

This discussion brings us to one of the most amazing types of equivalences that can be imagined, derived solely from string theory considerations, called the symmetry principle.

This principle—denoted by the simple equation $R = 1/R$, where R is the radius of our very large universe—is telling us that our huge universe (which is billions of light years across) is no different from a universe that is so tiny that it is inconceivably small; much smaller than even a photon. A universe with radius R is equivalent to a universe with radius 1/R. In other words, there is no difference between big and small![9]

We can relate this to a statement in the *Zohar* which reads: "He who is very small is very big, and he who is very big is very small."[10] What this statement implies is that a person who, in his own eyes,[11] is very small and very humble is actually very great from the perspective of the Almighty. In this world, which is the world of deceit, he may appear small, but in the world of truth, he is very big. And the opposite is also true, a person who in this world considers himself to be great and outstanding is actually very small in the world of truth and from the true perspective of the Almighty.

What the symmetry principle adds to this obvious interpretation of the *Zohar's* statement is that both sides are true—simultaneously! The usual interpretation is that if you consider yourself to be small, in truth you are big, and if you consider yourself to be big, in truth you are small. But, now we are saying that to be very small is to be very big. Both are true simultaneously. So symmetry suggests that we cannot actually tell the difference between the two things. Big and small are entirely equivalent. It is not just a question of perspective; they really are exactly the same. Again, this is the most counterintuitive result of modern physics. We usually think that we can tell the difference between big and small. Yet, here comes string theory and teaches us that we really cannot tell the difference between the two.

And when it comes to God, no matter what the perspective, being big or small makes no difference to Him. The main thing is to live a sincere life, with earnest intentions, as the infinitude of God makes us all small before Him.

Exponential Growth

Once our straight line was transformed into a dynamic three-dimensional hose, a world of possibilities opened up before us and we entered the realm of exponential growth. Now that we have traveled from a relatively-straight, one-dimensional consciousness to a three-dimensional one, we can begin to consider how many more dimensions we can "curl up" beneath us. And that brings us to the fourth and fifth types of effort—"one" (*echad*), called "a formed point" in Kabbalah, and "singular one" (*yachid*), called "an unformed point."

It is explained in rabbinic literature[12] that the first letter of the word "one" (echad—אֶחָד)—which is alef (א) and which has the numerical value of 1—stands for Alufo shel Olam—אַלוּפוֹ שֶׁל עוֹלָם, meaning the "Master of the World." The middle letter, chet (ח), which has the numerical value of 8, stands for the seven heavens and earth. And the last letter dalet (ד), which has the numerical value of 4, stands for the four spatial directions. Thus the word "one" implies that all of reality is permeated with the oneness of God.

So central is this theme that the primary declaration of our monotheistic faith—better known as the Shema—"Hear O' Israel, Havayah our God, Havayah is one" ends with this word "one."

Whereas the highest level of effort, "singular one" (yachid), is above and beyond reality, "one" (echad) enters and permeates all seven heavens, earth, and all four directions with the oneness of the "Master of the World."

While there are many levels of effort, the distinction is made by how each step forward changes reality. At the "one" level, all of the dimensions (both temporal and spatial) curl up under us with each step we take.

While each step forward is clearly defined—or, as Kabbalah would put it, is a "formed point"—the most important intention of this "one" mindset is to keep progressing on the journey. The hope is that each step forward will imbue all of reality with the oneness of God. The joy is in the knowledge that our positive efforts—our "one" steps forward—bring us closer to appreciating the oneness in all of creation. Just as a baby views each new step and observation as wondrous, so should our moments and days be filled with a sense of newfound wonder at the oneness to be found in creation. And we should view each step as starting from zero.[13]

Zero-Point

The level of "one" (*echad*) is still a lower consciousness than "singular one" (*yachid*) as it takes into account the various levels of creation—the seven heavens, earth, and the four spatial directions. It envisions oneness as the reflection of the one within the many. In contrast, the highest level of the "singular one"—or the "unformed point" as it is called in Kabbalah—expresses the absolute nullification of the many in the presence of the ultimate One.

In order to explain this level better, we first need to introduce the concept of a zero-point, or mid-point of nothingness, which exists at each level of consciousness.

There is a famous saying of the Ba'al Shem Tov, the founder of the Chassidic Movement, that "No matter what the innovation of any great rabbi, I can contradict it." This is truly a remarkable statement because in his time lived some very great sages. What then was the Ba'al Shem Tov trying to say by this? Clearly, he was not trying to make himself out to be smarter than everyone else. So how could he find a loophole in any new line of reasoning?

The Ba'al Shem Tov himself explained his meaning. He said that every theory that is proposed is a thought experiment in the realm of a particular world. But, in the middle-most point of that world, or that reality, lies an essential nothingness. There is only one great soul—called "the Moses of the generation"—that is in tune with this zero-point[14] and the Ba'al Shem Tov was in tune with that zero-point, and this is why he could contradict any theory.

The Ba'al Shem Tov understood that the points of nothingness at each level of consciousness are connected to one another. Together, all the zero-points through all the worlds are like a tube, or pillar, through which the person who is in tune with them can ascend and descend. This is a very deep and important realization for science in general and for us in particular, as we now consider the "singular one" level of effort.

"Singular one" (*yachid*) is the unformed or dimensionless zero-point in the middle of reality that sees only Divine Nothingness. A *tzadik* at this level can seamlessly travel from one dimension, world or theory to the next, because he's not caught up in any particular one. For this *tzadik*, everything is an infinite field or expanse of Godliness. No matter where he turns, he sees light and Divine revelation everywhere.[15]

It is because of this that a *tzadik* at the level of "singular one" may also think that his one step forward will take an entire lifetime since the effort isn't measurable to begin with. But even if he reaches a state of infinite effort (if such a thing is possible), then even that infinite effort can transition over to another level of infinity.

A story told by the holy Rebbe Yisrael of Ruzhin illustrates this point:

> When I was a young child, four years old, my holy father Rabbi Shalom of Prabitch took me on

a walk through the fields and there we saw the sun setting, a beautiful and grand sight. Watching the sunset, it seemed to me as a young boy that the place on the horizon where the sun was setting was the end of the sky. I told my father, "Look Abba, you can see where the sky ends." My father answered, "Know my child that beyond the sky that you can see there is another sky, and beyond that another sky, and there are skies without number, one after another. And beyond all the skies there is the great God that created them all." When my father spoke those words, my stomach began to churn. And that churning continues to this very day.[16]

Instead of viewing each step as if starting from zero, as in the previous level of "one," the level of "singular one" encompasses the entirety of one's being. When a student is at the point of complete frustration, when he has given up hope of completing the task, yet immediately perseveres with all his might, then he has expended "singular one" effort.

As long as the student views himself as traveling sequentially from one task to the next, then no matter what level of effort is expended it will be proportionate to the previous effort. But the selflessness needed to move forward between horizons takes a willingness to fully leave the previous horizon behind. Likewise, a student who is connected to this zero-point level of effort is willing to take on new challenges without consideration of previous achievements and tasks.

The Folded Paper

We'd like to bring one more allegory to help explain the interplay between effort on the level of "one" (*echad*) and the "singular one" (*yachid*).

The leap from one world or dimension to the next can be compared to a piece of paper folded in half. While the person on the first side doesn't see the other, by leaping around in the right direction, he will land there nonetheless. Using this same analogy, a hole punctured through the first side of the paper would make an easier or more direct pathway to the second.

In order to further elaborate on this, let's consider the following mathematical exercise:

Let's start with a piece of paper the size of a newspaper that is one thousandth of a centimeter thick (0.001 cm). When the paper is folded once the thickness becomes 0.002 cm, twice the original thickness. The third time makes it 0.004, the fourth

0.008. If we continue to fold it in half over and over again, after 10 folds, the width would be 2^{10} or 1.024 cm; 17 folds would make it 2^{17}, 131 cm or just over 4 feet; 25 folds or 2^{25} makes it 33,554 cm or just over 1,100 feet. The smaller the paper becomes, the exponentially taller the paper. After 48 times, the thickness is a staggering 1,749,004 miles!

While most people haven't managed to fold a paper more than 7 or 8 times, what is important for us is the concept behind the story—of making something smaller while at the same time making it exponentially bigger.

King David was a person who constantly diminished (or folded) himself, and so he became exponentially bigger or more kingly for his efforts. He traveled "circuit after circuit," and he also folded up those circles (so to speak), or curled up dimensions of reality into smaller spaces with each step he took.

The folded paper illustrates how the levels of *echad* and *yachid* work. If a paper could be folded an infinite number of times, it would have to be both infinitely thin and tall at the same time. Thus, the act of including all of creation—the seven heavens, earth, and four spatial directions—into one point could be viewed as a lesson in "paper folding." The smaller we become, the more "oneness" of the vast universe we can include with each step we take.

Whereas King David's lowliness relates to "folding" in our allegory, Moses teaches us how to punch through the zero-point of each of these folded or curled up dimensions of reality. Though this is indicative of transcendent or singular oneness, Moses-like figures can more easily travel through these levels and worlds than can the step-by-step figures akin to King David.[17] So while King David folds oneness, Moses travels through the mid-point of it.

To summarize:

Level of Effort	Level of Soul	Kabbalistic Terminology	Approach to Effort
Unformed Point	"Singular Soul" (Yechidah—יְחִידָה)	"Singular One" (Yachid—יָחִיד)	A person in-tune with Divine Nothingness who continuously leaps from one world to the next through the common zero-point
Formed Point	"Living Spirit" (Chayah—חַיָּה)	"One" (Echad—אֶחָד)	A person who takes wondrous new "baby steps" on his journey through life
Three-Dimensional Line	"Soul" (Neshamah—נְשָׁמָה)	"Primordial" (Kadmon—קַדְמוֹן)	A person who continually fits "squares into circles," by infusing more of his prior circular or static life, with a new sense of straightness or progress
Growth or Straight	"Spirit" (Ruach—רוּחַ)	"Straight" (Yosher—יוֹשֶׁר)	A person who invests new energy in his deeds, as the tzadik does maximally
Fixed or Circular	"Psyche" (Nefesh—נֶפֶשׁ)	"Cyclical" (Igulim—עִיגוּלִים)	A person who acts simply by inertia, in order to "get by" in life

9

THREE TYPES OF PRAISE

Praise Expanded

Now that we have explained the five levels of effort, we can go back to our original topic of praise and expand it beyond the scope of Dr. Dweck's theory.

We saw earlier that various elements of her diagram—challenges, obstacles, effort, accepting criticism and relating to the success of others—correspond to the four lower *sefirot* on the Kabbalistic Tree of Life. Now, we will take up the function of the three so-called emotive *sefirot* that reside above the lower, behavioral *sefirot*.[1] These are loving-kindness (*chesed*—חֶסֶד), might (*gevurah*—גְבוּרָה), and beauty (*tiferet*—תִּפְאֶרֶת).

keter — כֶּתֶר

"crown"

binah — בִּינָה   chochmah — חָכְמָה

"understanding"   "wisdom"

da'at — דַּעַת

"knowledge"

gevurah — גְּבוּרָה   chesed — חֶסֶד

"might"   "loving-kindness"

tiferet — תִּפְאֶרֶת

"beauty"

hod — הוֹד   netzach — נֶצַח

"acknowledgment"   "victory"

yesod — יְסוֹד

"foundation"

malchut — מַלְכוּת

"kingdom"

Dr. Dweck's theory of mindsets relates to "voluntary" or "operant" behavior patterns that are generated by the environment of the subject and that are maintained by consequences. Psychologists usually refer to the two extremes in behavior maintenance/modification as "reinforcement and punishment," or as "positive and negative" feedback. Participants in operant-conditioning experiments are given positive feedback to reinforce desired actions, or negative feedback to punish undesirable actions. Probably the best known example for this is in the behavioral training of lab rats which are rewarded with food for "positive" actions and punished with small electrical shocks for "negative" actions.

Voluntary or operant behaviors, according to Kabbalah, are a manifestation of *netzach, hod* and *yesod.* However, above these are three character-traits that Kabbalah calls the emotive attributes of the soul. These three are *chesed, gevurah,* and *tiferet.*

Emotions play an important role in inspiring us to act according to our soul-root. But while emotions consciously arouse us to act, the manifestation of the behavior should be in accordance with the behavioral *sefirot.* For while emotions are often full of conflict and compulsion, behavior ideally should express itself as natural and stable. It can then be seen as the constructive response to the enlightened emotions aroused in the heart.[2]

Practical Application: The Chocolate Bar

The practical result of the above insight is for parents and educators to focus on arousing or inspiring the emotions of each child towards positive actions. The hope is that from well-placed praises, the child will eventually learn to adopt positive behaviors that will serve him or her for the rest of life.

Integral to this approach is that a child should see praise as something dynamic or growth-oriented, and not the opposite. Praise is intended to encourage growth, not stifle it. In order to get this message across, a parent or educator should be well-versed in the three emotive attributes, for emotions are also motivated by reward and punishment. But instead of being something operant or voluntary, emotions are excitable and consciously motivate actions. The parent or educator wants to inspire the child to act in a certain way today, right now, not some time in the future. While these actions will hopefully become more ingrained as the child matures, it takes time to train a child to adopt a new pattern of behavior.

Let's now consider how this might work in practice by dissecting an example of a young child who has just been given a chocolate bar. If an educator sees the child give a piece of his chocolate bar to a friend, say a blessing before eating, and then sit down to learn now that his sweet tooth was satisfied, then the educator can praise all three emotions:

- *Chesed*—The educator can praise the child for having done a kind act by giving a piece of his chocolate bar to his friend. The educator can say: "You did a kind thing by giving some of that sweet chocolate to your friend."

- *Gevurah*—The inner-experience of "might" is "awe" or "fear." The educator can praise the child for having expressed "fear or Heaven" by saying a blessing: "Even though you probably wanted to take a bite right away, you stopped yourself and remembered to say a blessing."

- *Tiferet*—Torah learning corresponds to "beauty" as the Torah was given to the Jewish people by God with both the right hand of "loving-kindness" and the left hand of "might." The educator can praise the Torah that the child learned after satisfying his sweet tooth: "Now that your sweet tooth was satisfied, you have nourished yourself with Torah study, which is even sweeter!"[3]

A Soldier in God's Army

If praise is meant to be dynamic and encourage growth, then in order to keep it from degenerating into something static, it would be helpful to have a key image in mind that encapsulates this entire approach. That image, proposed by the Lubavitcher Rebbe, Rabbi Menachem Mendel Schneerson, is that of a soldier in the army of God. The Rebbe even founded a children's movement—for both boys and girls—called Tzivot Hashem ("The Army of God").

There are three primary characteristics required to be a soldier in this army: the first is that the soldier be a kind individual (*chassid*); the second that the soldier be "God fearing"; and the third that the soldier "study Torah diligently."[4]

How does this model motivate us to grow and move forward? It is a well-known acronym amongst chassidim that a "soldier" (*chayal*—חַיָל) is one that continuously goes "from strength to strength" (*m'chayil el chayil*—מֵחַיִל אֶל חָיִל).[5] If we want to be enlisted in this army, not only must we follow orders, we must also keep pushing ourselves further to do more than what we previously thought possible. Naturally, a soldier, or anyone who aims to progress from strength to strength, needs to keep moving forward.

Praising at the level of loving-kindness means to encourage all of the above as well to encourage loving-kindness. The intention behind this form of praise should be to reinstate the consciousness of God's abiding loving-kindness over all of creation.

At home or in the classroom, the simple message is that good acts help to fix the world (*tikkun olam*), or, as Maimonides says, a single good deed can spread loving-kindness over all of creation:

> Every man should view himself as equally balanced: half good and half evil. Likewise, he should see the entire world as half good and half evil... So that with a single good deed he will tip the scales for himself, and for the entire world, to the side of good.[6]

So when we praise a child for giving a piece of chocolate to his friend, we can say that he is like Abraham, emulating God who bestows kindness on creation, and that this one small act could be the "tipping point" needed to bring redemption to the world. To be sure, even a young child hearing these words will never view a chocolate bar in quite the same way again!

And this brings us to how the three emotive *sefirot* relate to our soul-root and to our physical bodies.[7]

Loving-Kindness in the Soul and in the Body

"Loving-kindness (*chesed*—חֶסֶד) is the first of the seven character attributes in the soul, and reflects the primary force that God employed in creating the world, as intimated by this verse in Psalms: "The world is constructed with loving-kindness."[8]

The inner essence or motivating force of *chesed* is "love" (*ahavah*—אַהֲבָה), the quality that causes us to relate to others with unconditional goodwill and benevolence.[9] Although each *sefirah* represents a power or ability latent in our personalities, loving-kindness can be seen as the force that moves us toward greatness—indeed, it is also called "greatness" (*gedulah*—גְּדוּלָה)[10]—for it nurtures our character by promoting the total development of our being.[11]

Our father Abraham is identified in the Torah with all three of these concepts: *chesed*, *ahavah* and *gedulah* as demonstrated by the following verses:

- *Chesed:* "You shall give truth of Jacob, loving-kindness of Abraham, which You swore to our forefathers from days of yore." [12]

- *Ahavah:* "But you, Israel My servant, Jacob whom I have chosen, the seed of Abraham, who loved Me."[13]

- *Gedulah:* "And the name of Hebron before was Kiryat Arba, the City of Arba. This man [Arba, i.e., Abraham] was the greatest man among the giants. And the land had rest from war."[14]

The numerical value of Abraham's name (248) is equivalent to the number of positive, active commandments of the Torah. And to love God means to lovingly fulfill all of the 248 active commandments of the Torah.[15] As well, the number 248 is equivalent to the number of bones in the body.[16] Thus loving-kindness, the attribute of Abraham, is identified with the skeletal system in the body and may well serve as a spiritual remedy for skeletal diseases.[17]

The phrase in the Torah "the God of Abraham,"[18] is understood in Kabbalah to refer to the overarching, Divine life-force above loving-kindness (with Abraham as the archetypal soul)—which is the intellectual faculty of wisdom (chochmach—חָכְמָה) directly above the emotive attribute of loving-kindness on the right axis of the Kabbalistic Tree of Life. The bones of the body act as the vessels or containers for the bone marrow. Thus, the physiological analogy to the spiritual level referred to as "the God of Abraham" is the system of the bone marrow (that creates blood cells) above and within the system of the skeleton.

Might in the Soul and in the Body

The second of the emotive attributes is the *sefirah* of "might" (*gevurah*—גְּבוּרָה). This trait is also associated with the power of "judgment" (*din*—דִּין). In the workings of creation, judgment represents an opposing force of constriction, in contrast to the expansive force of loving-kindness. In effect, *gevurah* seeks to preserve the intrinsic boundaries which God set for each and every element within creation.

The inner essence of might is "awe" (*yirah*—יִרְאָה).[19] Awe represents the trepidation in the soul that holds a person back from indiscriminately showering kindness upon others. Whereas love, the inner essence of loving-kindness, impels a person to give unconditionally, awe argues against giving in this manner. While the deserving nature of the recipient is taken into account for an awe-inspired giver, such considerations are not weighed for a giver intent on showering boundless love and generosity upon others.

However, an awe-inspired person agrees with the love-inspired person that everyone should receive their just reward, even in the face of overwhelming opposition. Should Divine justice dictate that someone be extended a particular benefit, a person inspired by fear or awe of heaven does everything possible to facilitate it. Consequently, the antithetical position that *gevurah* takes vis-à-vis *chesed* actually serves to promote the ultimate good. Concerned with maintaining the proper measure, *gevurah* works to defend the boundaries of judgment, while allowing the appropriate measure of loving-kindness.

To put it another way, *gevurah* makes sure that everyone gets 100% of what they are entitled to, while remembering that what is Divinely apportioned varies from person to person. *Gevurah* establishes the rigorous standard of merit that ensures that the subsequent beneficence of *chesed* is bestowed with genuine value and meaning for each recipient. Thus *gevurah* works hand-in-hand with *chesed*—as it says in the Talmud, "the left arm [of *gevurah*] pushes away while the right arm [of *chesed*] draws near." [20]

In the body, it is the property of *gevurah*—located on the left axis of the Tree of Life directly below the *sefirah* of "understanding" (*binah*—בִּינָה) which itself corresponds to blood—to control blood's circulation throughout the body. *Gevurah* channels the blood and directs it into the specific blood vessels of the circulatory system (which it creates).

According to Kabbalah, there are 365 major blood vessels in the human body which correspond to the 365 prohibitive commandments of the Torah.[21] The 365 blood vessels also correspond to the 365 days of the solar year. Each one of these blood vessels includes both an artery and its related vein. The distinction between arteries and veins is as follows: the arteries (which pulsate as they carry oxygenated blood) are likened to the days of the year (which are characterized by activity/pulsation), while the veins (which do not pulsate as they return oxygen-depleted blood) are likened to the nights (which are characterized by rest). Each complete blood vessel thus includes a full circuit—both a day and a night.

While we might regard the blood and blood vessels as a single system, it can also be regarded as two separate physiological systems similar to what we described above in relation to the bone marrow and the skeleton).[22] Similar to the duality of day and night within each blood vessel, according to Kabbalah the light of a blood vessel is the blood, whereas the vessel itself is the vessel needed to hold the light contained within the blood.

In Chassidic thought, the force of might/contraction that the blood vessels exert on the blood itself serves to strengthen the life-force inherent in the blood.[23]

Contraction is an act of "might," the basic meaning of *gevurah*. As mentioned, its inner experience is awe in the presence of God and fear of the consequences of disobeying Him. With awe comes the power to control and direct the life-force that flows through the body in the form of blood. [24]

The archetypal soul in the Torah that personifies *gevurah* is Isaac, who lived a full life of 180 years— that is, 180 "days" (summers) and 180 "nights" (winters), completing a full cycle of 360 degrees. A healthy circulatory system is thus dependent upon "the fear/awe of Isaac,"[25] the source of might in the soul.

Practical Application: The Chocolate Bar Continued

Let's return to our example of the child eating a chocolate bar. How should we praise him in light of our discussion of *gevurah*?

Earlier we mentioned that he displayed the fear of God when he said a blessing before he took that first bite. The simple interpretation is that postponing enjoyment for a child is no easy task, so we make sure to acknowledge the fact that his consciousness of God took precedence over the delicious treat before him. But in a deeper sense, this act of "withholding" typifies the *gevurah* experience.

As we explained, a *gevurah*-inspired educator doesn't say that the child shouldn't eat the chocolate bar. Instead, his concern is mainly that the chocolate should come to the child in the appropriate way and in the appropriate measure. In addition to supervising how the child says a blessing before taking the first bite, the awe-inspired educator also analyzes whether the child did enough to merit receiving the chocolate to begin with, and even then, how much to actually give. The end result should leave the child feeling content that his chocolate came well-deserved and in an amount that makes him happy—enough to satisfy him, but not so much that he cannot consume it all and ends up wasting some.

As the child enjoys his chocolate, he also enjoys the praise that comes from his teacher who applauds his postponing his enjoyment to say a blessing and, in so doing, also helps him to take an active part in rectifying creation through his exhibition of proper restraint. This is an essential part of *tikkun olam* (fixing the world).

One way to explain this to a child is to say that sin is the result of impulsivity, as with Adam and Eve who were unable to wait three hours until the onset of the first Shabbat, at which time the forbidden fruit of the

Tree of Knowledge would have been permitted to them; but this child, by forcing himself to wait and make a blessing before he eats his chocolate, is fixing their mistake and developing the quality of restraint in the process.

While the world was created with *chesed*, this came after God's initial intention to create the world with *gevurah*. So while compassion and loving-kindness were the end result, there is something more primordial about might. Keeping this in mind, the teacher should be conscious of the fact that the child shouldn't need the chocolate bar at all to be conscious of God. But as the world we live in was built with loving-kindness, we still give him a chocolate bar today, with the hope that in the future, when he grows up, it will no longer be necessary.

Beauty in the Soul and in the Body

The third and final emotive attribute in the soul is the *sefirah* of "beauty" (*tiferet*—תִּפְאֶרֶת). The root of the Hebrew word for this *sefirah*—פ-א-ר—spells one of the eight synonyms for "beauty"[26] and refers specifically to the harmonious blending of various colors and forms.

Positioned along the central axis of the Tree of Life model of the *sefirot*, *tiferet* is the Divine power within creation which allows us to express a harmonious blend of the two opposites of *chesed* and *gevurah*. The inner essence that inspires beauty is "compassion" (*rachamim*—רַחֲמִים), which itself is composed of two aspects—an outer and an inner.

The outer aspect synthesizes the opposite elements of love and fear into a force of discriminating compassion. The result is a reasoned advocacy directed at those worthy and deemed capable of receiving compassion. In effecting an acceptable compromise between the counter-tendencies of love and fear, *rachamim* nonetheless favors love. This reflects the principle stated in Kabbalah that *tiferet* always tends toward the right, or the side of *chesed*.[27]

In its inner aspect, however, *rachamim* transcends this blending process and expresses itself as a power unrelated to and autonomous of the opposing forces of love and fear. In this respect, *rachamim* is the raw, empathic impulse that compels a person to respond compassionately to the pain of others. Stemming from a level higher than either the altruism of *chesed* or the restraint of *gevurah*, the inner spirit of compassion—and therefore of *tiferet*—is oblivious to reasoned arguments militating against such a response. Perhaps this is why, in the body, *tiferet* corresponds to the heart as well as the entire muscular system of the body.

The heart, which belongs both to the muscular system as well as to the circulatory system, tends to the left side of the body, alluding to the combined forces of both *tiferet* and *gevurah*. In general, a sound, well-developed muscular system makes for a beautiful body. Muscles are the seat of the body's physical strength. Here also, we see the combined forces of the spiritual attributes of *tiferet* and *gevurah*.

As mentioned, the inner experience of *tiferet* is compassion. In Kabbalah, we are taught that the Divine soul is expressed most potently in the attribute of compassion, for its power to choose good comes from its property of knowledge (*da'at*—דַעַת). (Note that *tiferet* appears directly below the intellectual *sefirah* of *da'at* on the middle axis of the Tree of Life and is informed by it.) This characteristic of the Divine soul is in contrast to the animal soul which lacks the faculty of knowledge; its expression of mercy toward others is mere pity, and it is unable to bring the feeling of compassion to actualization.

Potent compassion begins with a sense of true empathy for others, and it gives us the strength of character necessary to succeed in extending our hand to those in trouble. On the spiritual plane, potent compassion reflects a strong heart and a strong muscular system.

The intention, at this third emotively-inspired level, is that the educator should compassionately wean students away from a dependency on *chesed*, while not exhibiting the full force of *gevurah*. The students should feel that the teacher truly cares and empathizes with them and that any withholding of praise is for their own benefit.

In our chocolate bar example, praising the child for learning Torah—and pointing out to him that learning is even sweeter than the chocolate bar he consumed—may actually take away some of the physical enjoyment he experienced from the treat. But the caring educator, with a wide smile and caring eyes, is obviously teaching the importance of spiritual sweets over physical sweets. So while not taking the chocolate bar away completely, the caring educator knows how to properly wean the child away from the dependency on physical pleasures, while inculcating proper growth lessons.

As we mentioned before, the Torah itself corresponds to "beauty," as it was given to the Jewish people by God with both the hand of "loving-kindness" on the right and "might" on the left. Praising Torah study then should be done with both hands, so the student feels both loved and taken care of. Just like the body needs a healthy heart to function properly, a compassionate educator can help set his students on the correct pathway toward growth.

To summarize:

Properties	Demonstrated by	Soul Attribute	In Action	In the Body	Praise and Motivation
Emotive Properties	A Kind Individual	Loving-kindness (chesed—חֶסֶד)	One who acts with loving-kindness toward others	The Skeletal System	Praising to Inspire the Emotions
	A God-Fearing Individual	Might (gevurah—גְבוּרָה)	One who is God fearing and says a blessing before eating	The Circulatory System	
	A Scholar	Beauty (tiferet—תִפְאֶרֶת)	One who studies Torah realizing that the learning is even sweeter than physical delights.	The Muscular System	

Properties	Demonstrated by	Soul Attribute	In Action	In the Body	Praise and Motivation
Behavioral Properties	Challenges	Victory (netzach—נֵצַח)	One who rises to accept challenges	The Endocrine System	Behavior Training
	Obstacles	Acknowledgement (hod—הוֹד)	One who has the strength required to continually overcome obstacles	The Immune System	
	Effort	Foundation (yesod—יְסוֹד)	One who grows through effort	The Reproductive System	
	Appearance	The Crown of the Reproductive Organ (ateret hayesod—עֲטֶרֶת הַיְסוֹד)	One who has the desire to shine new light to the world	The Integumentary (Skin) System	
Feminine Properties	Accepting Criticism	Kingdom (malchut—מַלְכוּת)	One who is lowly enough to receive criticism	The Digestive System	Praising the ongoing results of the above
	Relating to the Success of Others		One who is willing to learn from everyone		

10

ACTION, SPEECH AND THOUGHT

The Three Garments of the Soul

Now that we have examined the seven lower *sefirot*, we arrive at their actual expression in the world—the so called "garments of the soul" of which there are three:

- "thought" (*machshavah*—מַחֲשָׁבָה)
- "speech" (*dibur*—דִּבּוּר) and
- "action" (*ma'aseh*—מַעֲשֶׂה)

These three vehicles of self-expression enable the powers of the soul to manifest in reality. Whereas speech and thought subdivide into two separate manifestations (as we will presently explain), action retains a single and unified expressive character. As will become clearer later on, we have chosen to begin our examination with action.

Action

Unlike speech and thought, action does not branch into two derivative modes of conduct. The essence of physical action is the pursuit of a direct and unmediated involvement with the outside world. Regardless of how that involvement is executed, deeply or superficially, the essential act remains the same. Such distinctions as are normally attached to our actions—labeling them good or evil, for example—derive from an external value-system that exists independent of the action itself. The action remains nothing more than a mute demonstration of creation interacting with itself.[1]

Although action is intrinsically void of the personal meaning that one attaches to it, it nevertheless paradoxically allows one to leave a unique mark upon creation. Whereas the garments of thought and speech are inseparably identified with the soul that produces them, they nevertheless disappear from reality unless captured through some objective action, such as writing. However, with action, it makes no difference who is the actor. The main thing is that the act gets done.

The ultimate vehicle for constructive self-expression is the act of performing a mitzvah. The democratic nature of action—equally accessible to all regardless of stature—makes the mitzvah the great equalizer of Jewish experience and the ideal platform for demonstrating the unity of Israel.

Possessing great intelligence or spiritual depth does not qualify a particular individual's mitzvah as any more real or significant than that of another with lesser qualities. By engaging all Jews in a common physical dialogue with creation, performance of a mitzvah allows everyone to serve as a vehicle for expressing the indistinct unity throughout creation.[2]

It should be noted, that while action is democratic in nature, there are parameters in the Torah specifying whom to give to and whom not to give to. For instance, a person should not give charity to a cruel enemy.

Speech

The garment of speech is a mode of self-expression that involves verbally sharing our thoughts and feelings with others. However, there are two fundamentally different styles of communication which are termed in Kabbalah "words spoken from the heart" and "words that issue only from the lips and outward."

In truth, all speech is an attempt to project ourselves into reality. Just as the extent to which our voice projects depends upon the depth from which it originates, so too, the identity conveyed by our voice manifests itself differently, depending on whether we speak from the heart or merely with our lips.[3]

Insofar as the deeper significance behind creation remained camouflaged until the revelation at Mt. Sinai, the ten supreme utterances that brought the universe into being were merely a kind of Divine "lip service." Without the disclosure at Sinai of God's program for creation, man's existence would have remained superficial and barren of genuine meaning.

However, God needed to adequately prepare the world to receive the import of His Torah. Our sages teach us that "words spoken from the heart penetrate the heart."[4] Without a heart properly prepared, the conveyance of Divine Essence at the time of creation would have been in vain. However, the situation at Sinai was markedly different. From that first moment of Israel's gathering at the mountain, God set about fashioning the heart of a people to be ready to receive the most profound revelation of the Divine to mankind.

Thought

While action and speech are modes of expression that relate to others, the primary purpose of thought is the achievement of self-enlightenment. As with speech, thought also breaks down into two distinct levels: the first is "focused thought" and the second is "random reflection."

Focused thought is the capacity for concentrated and penetrating analysis that proceeds through layer after layer of intellectual understanding. In contrast, random reflection is free-flowing and non-critical thought which, though lacking in focus and depth, is rich in associative imagery. If left totally untamed, this perpetual drift of thought could cause the cognitive powers to diffuse, leaving the soul feeling lost. However, when harnessed in the service of meaningful contemplation, drifting thoughts can enable us to discover new horizons that we may never have glimpsed through the discipline of focused thought alone.

Chocolate Bar Example

Here is how we can understand praise of the child eating the chocolate bar in terms of the three garments of the soul we have been discussing:

- *Garment of Action*: When we praise a child for being a kind and generous person because he gave a piece of chocolate to his friend, our intention is that this praise should inspire the child to do another good deed next time.

- *Garment of Speech*: When we praise a child for restraining himself from taking that first sweet bite, for being conscious of God and saying a blessing, our hope is that more God-fearing speech should come from his mouth in the future.

- *Garment of Thought*: When we praise a child for studying Torah after he eats his piece of chocolate and tell him that learning is even sweeter than the physical delight he just consumed, we are training him to progress to a point where he won't need candy in order to learn.

What we have just done here is to extend Dweck's mindsets diagram by another three categories. Our point is that, for praise to be effective, it needs to inspire the child toward actualizing one of these three garments. If it is either speech or thought, the hope is that the child will be inspired to choose the inner dimension of each and turn it into action.

While a blessing counts even if the child recites it without intent, it is best that he consciously thinks about God during the blessing. The hope of an educator is that praise—in this case the praise given to encourage the child to say a blessing the next time—is that the child should say the blessing from the inner intentions of his heart.

Likewise, when an educator praises a student's thoughtful Torah study even if the child was not concentrating all the while, the educator hopes that the praise will encourage the child to eventually pursue more in-depth modes of study.

In addition to being the manifestation of the three categories of emotive-inspired praise, there is something else that the garments of the soul—thought, speech and action—teach us. That is, that we don't need to be overly concerned with praising intelligence. While praising a child for utilizing his intelligence in the study of Torah, the first thing we try to praise is the act of kindness, then speech and finally thought/intelligence.

Small Acts of Kindness

If given the choice, we praise the action that was performed over the thoughts or spoken words because a single good deed can tip the entire world to the side of good, as we noted previously from Maimonides.

Even when praising speech—for example, a blessing—we tell the child how clearly he recited it. While we hope that praise will inspire God-conscious intentions in his heart, the praise is focused on the action. Partially this is because we cannot know the intentions in the heart and mind of the child. But, in addition to this, as the Lubavitcher Rebbe said many times, "action is the main thing." Meaning that even if we believe that the child is thinking or praying with great intention and effort, we should focus on the end result.

While we need to be careful to train a child away from superficial or perfunctory acts, still this shouldn't hold us back from acknowledging any good action for, no matter how weak the intent, it is still worthy of being praised for what it is: an action.

The action of giving charity (*tzedakah*—צְדָקָה) is such an important good deed that whenever the Jerusalem Talmud uses the word "mitzvah" without stating which mitzvah it means, it is assumed to be referring to *tzedakah*. And the Babylonian Talmud states, "If a person gives even a *prutah* (the tiniest coin) to the poor, he merits and receives the presence of God."[5]

It is explained in Chassidut that, whereas other good deeds are performed with specific limbs of the body, the good deed of giving *tzedakah* conditions all our limbs to a life of kindness and generosity. Just like we use all our limbs in order to earn our livelihood, so too, the act of giving away our hard-earned money is done through the effort of the entire body.

The word *tzedakah* (צְדָקָה) shares its Hebrew root with *tzedek* (צֶדֶק) meaning "justice"; this implies that *tzedakah* promotes the just redistribution of nature's bounty amongst all His creatures who equally deserve its benefit.

Also, as mentioned before in the explanation of the *sefirah* of *malchut*, it doesn't matter whom God chose to be the "cursor on the screen" that day; the point is that the good action gets done, no matter whose name is "signed at the bottom." In *tzedakah*, this approach relates to the anonymity associated with the act itself. The highest level of charitable giving is when neither the giver nor the receiver are aware of each other's identity.

Eventually, every one of us should ingrain this "anonymity" in every good action that we do. The identification between the doer and the deed is the act itself. We should feel that we are doing this good deed because this is what God wants from us at this moment, not because we felt the need to do something good.

The feeling of self-importance steers us into a fixed mindset. When we feel that our natural talents and abilities are what sets us apart from and above others, then the "good" that we do is only a form of self-aggrandizement. But as we learned from the lowliness exhibited by King David, if even a king of Israel can view his role as a mere "custodian" of the task at hand, certainly so should we.

This does not mean that we can't be motivated to succeed and move forward in life. As we mentioned when discussing King David, it is actually the opposite. Once we free ourselves from the hold of our own ego, then the ego's distraction methods of success and failure no longer work. Since it is God doing the action through us, the end result is not up to us.

Dr. Dweck explains the success/failure trap as follows:

> Yes, children love praise. And they especially love to be praised for their intelligence and talent. It really does give them a boost, a special glow—but only for the moment. The minute they hit a snag, their confidence goes out the window and their motivation hits rock bottom.

> If success means they're smart, then failure means they're dumb. That's the fixed mindset.[6]

As we saw in the story of the community rabbi who lost his job, the success/failure trap is not something that only children fall into. The ego doesn't care who it is, as long as it fosters a fixed mindset.

The challenge for the educator is to wean children away from the "standardized test score" mentality. Even a student who gets a perfect 100% on the test could be failing a very important lesson in life. The same goes for the students who think they are failing, but perhaps happens to just think differently and in a uniquely creative way than what the test can detect. What matters is how students apply the talents and abilities they have, and how they persevere amidst challenges and obstacles, not how they score or perform relative to their classmates.

11

PRAISING INTELLIGENCE

When is Intelligence Praiseworthy?

The most important task for a parent or educator is to praise the goodness in the heart of the child. Next comes the child's fear of Heaven, and then finally their intelligence. But even when intelligence is praised, the child should know that it is not the essence of life.

When a child is praised for doing a good deed, then there is no danger of creating a fixed mindset. Ideally, when an educator praises a good deed, it should lead to even greater good deeds for, as previously noted, *chesed* is equated with greatness, which in turn is synchronized with the growth mindset.

Whereas people try to assess intelligence using IQ tests or some other measurements, the only thing that limits a good deed is a person's own sense of involvement with the act itself. Whereas intelligence has standardized tests and measures, there is a no accurate test to see how kind a person truly is.

Unlike acts of kindness and even God-fearing speech, intelligence presents itself as out of our control. In the language of Chassidut, whereas the garments of action and speech "detach" when we are not acting or speaking, our thoughts are always constantly running. For a growth mindset individual, who wants to focus on changing his "garments" for the better, the easiest thing to start with is the most easily "detachable garment" of action.

However, there are times when intelligence deserves to be praised—and that is when it is used for the purpose it was given. As the Prophet Jeremiah states:

> So says God, "The wise man should not praise his wisdom; the mighty should not praise his might; the wealthy shall not praise his wealth. For only in this shall he who is praised be praised: in contemplating and knowing Me, for I, God, practice loving-kindness, justice and *tzedakah* (charity/righteousness) on the earth. For in these things I delight," says God.[1]

From this we learn that it is praiseworthy to use intelligence, as long as the goal is to know God, in order to emulate His ways.

Dr. Dweck also agrees that the wise should not praise his wisdom, the mighty his might, and the wealthy his wealth. Even if in the past the person had to work hard to attain these attributes, now that he has them, it is of utmost importance that he not fall into a state of complacency.

But Jeremiah is telling us something more—that by recognizing what these gifts are for, a person can stay on the path of growth. If a person was born intelligent, then it was in order to know God.

The implication from this is that being intelligent doesn't make a person any better off. To the contrary, as we have seen throughout history, it has been the "smart" people who have caused the most strife and bloodshed in the world. What matters most is that each person's talents and abilities are properly directed. If the talent is intelligence, then this gift should be used to know God and emulate God.

The Realm of the Intellect

In this chapter, we have begun to introduce yet another three levels to Dweck's mindsets diagram, levels which correspond to the three intellectual *sefirot* of "wisdom" (*chochmach*—חׇכְמָה), "understanding" (*binah*—בִּינָה) and "knowledge" (*da'at*—דַּעַת).

keter—כֶּתֶר

"crown"

binah—בִּינָה	*chochmah*—חׇכְמָה
"understanding"	"wisdom"

da'at—דַּעַת

"knowledge"

gevurah—גְבוּרָה	*chesed*—חֶסֶד
"might"	"loving-kindness"

tiferet—תִּפְאֶרֶת

"beauty"

hod—הוֹד	*netzach*—נֶצַח
"acknowledgment"	"victory"

yesod—יְסוֹד

"foundation"

malchut—מַלְכוּת

"kingdom"

We shall now focus our discussion on the three intellectual levels of praise. To be sure, once an educator learns how to praise at the level of the intellect, then praising properly at the emotional and behavioral levels will flow from there.[2]

As noted several times thus far, the essence of proper praise is to be able to distinguish between good and bad praise—that is, between praise which fosters a growth mindset and that which inhibits it. And the ability to distinguish between the two begins with the three intellectual *sefirot*.

If an educator is correctly praising at the level of the intellect, then she will be correct at the other levels as well. Indeed, this is how the verse from Jeremiah concludes: "For I, God, practice loving-kindness, justice and *tzedakah* (charity/righteousness) on the earth."

The reference to the three emotive *sefirot* is clear: "loving-kindness" (*chesed*—חֶסֶד) obviously relates to the *sefirah* of *chesed*; "judgment" (*mishpat*—מִשְׁפָּט) is a clear reference to the *sefirah* of *gevurah*; and "charity/righteousness" (*tzedakah*—צְדָקָה) corresponds to the *sefirah* of *tiferet* because to compassionately give charity is the fullest expression of the emotions of the heart.

As was done previously, we will now explain each of the three intellectual *sefirot* as they are experienced both in the soul and in the body. Along the way, we will also relate back to the type of praise associated with each.

Wisdom in the Soul and the Body

The *sefirah* of *chochmah* is the father-principle at work in the intellect. It is the innovative and essentially unpredictable force that produces those spontaneous insights which we nurture to maturity through the companion power of *binah*, the mother-principle of intelligence.

The inner experience of *chochmah* is "self-nullification" (*bitul*—בִּטּוּל). In Kabbalah, the Hebrew word for wisdom—חָכְמָה—is often explained as the transposition of the two words כֹּחַ מַה (*koach mah*) meaning "the power of what [i.e. nothing]."[3]

The result of absenting our ego from the equation allows us to fully acknowledge and affirm the Divine Source to which we are ultimately connected. By grafting our consciousness to the ground of all being, we become conduits for Divine wisdom, which expresses itself through flashes of spontaneous intuitive insight. As bolts of lightning, these flashes of insight may lack permanence but, nevertheless, they serve to spark our subsequent pursuit of meaningful knowledge.

The verse from Jeremiah, quoted earlier, begins with *chochmah* by stating that a wise man should not be praised for his wisdom if he views it as his own. This is a lesson for a student who experiences a flash of insight—especially a new insight in his Torah learning. He should know that since God and the Torah are one,[4] his insight is not his at all. As a result of the diligence and effort which he has expended in his studies, he was given this insight as a gift from Above.

The challenge at this level of praise is that only an accomplished mentor can know whether or not to praise the student for innovation in his Torah learning. The purpose and the result of the praise is not that the student should feel that he is smart, but that he has developed a correct contact point with God.

If the mentor is well-versed in praising at the level of *chochmah*, then his student will have the wonderful opportunity to be open to more insights and Divine connections.

In the body, the *sefirah* of *chochmah* corresponds to the bone marrow. Current medical research regards bone marrow as a system in its own right.[5] As previously stated, bone marrow is responsible for producing blood cells, the most basic biological unit in the body. Just as every aspect of the body depends on the bone marrow, so too, all of existence depends on wisdom, as King David teaches us: "[God,] You have made all [of Your creations] with wisdom."[6]

A lack of insightfulness may indicate a weak bone marrow system. The answer lies in the devoted study of the inner dimension of the Torah, namely Kabbalah and Chassidut, which awakens the soul's innate faculty of wisdom.

The production of blood cells from the bone marrow resembles, on the physical plane, a creative process of *ex nihilo*, "something from nothing." On the spiritual plane, experiencing oneself continuously being created *ex nihilo* may well serve to strengthen one's bone-marrow system.

Understanding in the Soul and the Body

The *sefirah* of *binah* is the cognitive force that absorbs the nuclear seed of wisdom and articulates it into fine detail through a process of associative analysis referred to as "understanding one thing from another."[7]

This process of understanding entails more than just deductively extracting a model of reality from the shorthand of wisdom; it also involves the ability to intuit a more inclusive reality than what is encoded within wisdom itself. Once having attained the mature understanding of *binah*, the soul swells with delight at its achievement. The inner experience of *binah* is thus identified in Chassidut as "joy" (*simchah*—שִׂמְחָה). Joy is the essential response of the soul to a feeling of accomplishment. Indeed, the very word in Hebrew for "accomplishment" (*hasagah*—הַשָּׂגָה) is generally associated with intellectual achievement, particularly the kind represented by *binah*'s elaboration of *chochmah* into full-bodied constructions of thought.

The male and female *sefirot* of *chochmah* and *binah* are depicted in the *Zohar* as "two inseparable companions." Every thought we experience is predicated upon the collaboration between these two cognitive principles. When we find each of them expressed in Kabbalah as an autonomous conceptual structure (*partzuf*—פַּרְצוּף), they are referred to as "father" (*aba*—אַבָּא) and "mother" (*ima*—אִמָּא). Their sustained interaction is the precondition for the subsequent birth in the soul of character attributes, appropriately called "children" in Kabbalah.[8]

Earlier we mentioned that the *sefirah* of *binah* relates to the ability to appreciate finer details through the associative analysis process referred to as "understanding one thing from another." Therefore, a student should not be praised at this level if he merely elaborated on a concise statement, but only when he was able to intuit a more inclusive reality than what was originally encoded within wisdom itself. Within this larger picture of reality he perceives new details. *Binah* is the ability to see and to analyze every new detail and to select the appropriate action as a result of this analysis. That is what is worthy of being praised. An example of this in the Torah world is a *posek*, an adjudicator of Jewish laws, who when presented with a new situation (one that was not addressed explicitly by the sages of previous generations) is skilled in choosing the correct decision from many possible options (based upon past decisions, but seeing them through the lens of a larger reality, that which includes the innovations of the present times). Central to this level is also that this process be undertaken for the sake of Heaven.

While we spoke previously about the praise of prayer, this type of praise has not yet entered our expanded version of the mindsets diagram. Although we mentioned that praising a child who remembers to say a blessing corresponds to the *sefirah* of *gevurah* (because the child restrained himself from eating and recited the blessing first), the actual source of prayer is the *sefirah* of *binah*.

Located directly above *gevurah* on the left axis of the Kabbalistic Tree of Life, the *sefirah* of *binah* (בִּינָה) shares its Hebrew root with the word *hitbonenut* (הִתְבּוֹנְנוּת) meaning "meditation." When we speak of meditation in this sense, we speak of the contemplative study of Chassidut that precedes morning prayers. This follows perfectly with the alignment of the *sefirot*, with *binah* descending to beget *gevurah* as one of the "six children" that are born from the union of *chochmah* and *binah*.

In the body, the *sefirah* of *binah* is associated with the blood itself, now also considered a physiological system in its own right, in addition to the circulatory system of the blood vessels. *Binah* (בִּינָה) which shares its Hebrew root with the verb "build" (*banah*—בָּנָה), receives its raw material from *chochmah*, the bone marrow, building upon its encoded information.

In Kabbalah, *binah* is referred to as the "mother," whose primary contributions to the formation of her child are the red aspects of his or her body. In contrast, *chochmah* is referred to as the "father," who generates the white aspects of the body, such as the bones.[9] Of the mother, it is said, "the mother of the children is joyful."[10] A lack of joy in life may reflect a problem in the blood.[11] In Chassidut, we are taught that a deep, inner sense of joy comes from meditating on how the Divine Providence watches over all creation. Similar to the effect of the blood on the limbs of the body, Divine Providence links together all creations so that they experience themselves as one organism. With the sense of God's care for all comes joy. Divine Providence channels Divine life-force to each of God's creations which flows as blood in a living organism, moving freely from one to another, from the healthy limb to heal the diseased limb. The joy of witnessing Divine Providence in one's life may thus serve to cure ailments relating to the blood.

These two relatively abstract physiological systems—the bone marrow and the blood—assume the roles of "father" and "mother" in the body and function together in perfect union. In Kabbalah, the continual union of the "father" and "mother" principles is responsible for the ongoing creation of reality, as the Zohar states: "the father [here, the bone marrow] and the mother [here, the blood] are two partners that never separate."[12] Their union, expressing the inner creative power of the living soul, is continuous, as illustrated by the fact that the bone marrow continuously creates new blood cells.

Knowledge in the Soul and the Body

The *sefirah* of *da'at*—the final Divine power to manifest itself through the intellect—is unusual insofar that it is only counted as one of the ten *sefirot* when "crown" (*keter*—כֶּתֶר) is not considered.[13] This is because the *sefirot* of *keter* and *da'at* represent two alternative expressions of a single Divine force: that which enables the soul to sustain diametrically opposite states of being at the same time.[14] Indeed, the term used to describe the inner essence of knowledge in the soul is "unification" (*yichud*—יְחוּד). As opposed to being another stage in the elaboration of the intellect, *da'at* signifies the power to unify and bridge (in the mind as well as in the heart) the conception of truth that one has already technically achieved through wisdom and understanding.

It is this power to penetrate and attach oneself to reality (which is the basis of memory as well) that enables a person to convert understanding into a force that vitalizes and inspires the character attributes as well as achieves expression through action and deed.

Since *da'at* is the connecting level between both inner and outer reality and the intellect and emotions, the praise that is offered at this level is intended to promote the positive "unions" between two opposite states that the student has made. This is called in the verse from Jeremiah "knowing Me." Even though there seems to be an infinite expanse between ourselves and God, an inner sensitivity at this level trains one to experience the Divine Providence at play in every aspect of creation. The end result, the quality that educators should hope to bring out in their students, is that they have used their faculty of knowledge to know God in order to emulate His ways.

In the body, the faculty of knowledge corresponds to the nervous system. Knowledge is understood in Kabbalah to be the seat of all of the soul's sensitivity and feeling. The body's sensors are its nerves. In Kabbalah, we are taught that knowledge possesses two seemingly antithetical but ultimately complementary sides. The first appearance of knowledge in the Torah is in reference to "the Tree of Knowledge of Good and Evil." From this we understand that knowledge is a sense of spiritual or moral polarity. The soul's power to sense good and to be attracted to it is referred to as the "right side" of knowledge, whereas the soul's power to sense evil and to repel it is referred to as the "left side" of knowledge. In a rectified soul, the attraction to good entails conscious self-awareness of loving the good;

whereas the soul's fear of evil, which is responsible for repelling and fighting off the evil, operates at an unconscious level.

When we abstract and extend this idea, we see that the right side of knowledge corresponds to all of the conscious sensations and voluntary reactions, while the left side of knowledge corresponds to all the unconscious sensations and involuntary reactions.

In terms of the nervous system in the body, the right side of knowledge corresponds to the voluntary nervous system, called the cerebrospinal system. Here, conscious sensation and control of the body implies self-awareness, or knowing oneself. In a rectified personality, knowing oneself is necessary in order for the individual to act constructively in the world and help others. For this reason, this side of knowledge is identified with the right.

The left side of knowledge corresponds to the involuntary nervous system, the autonomic nervous system, which itself divides into the sympathetic and parasympathetic systems. The parasympathetic system serves to slow the heart, dilate the blood vessels, increase the activity of the glands, constrict the pupils of the eyes and so forth, whereas the sympathetic system does the opposite.

Serving as the unconscious side of knowledge, the involuntary nervous system allows all of the body's necessary functions to perform automatically. Naturally occurring processes such as digestion and respiration function without a person's conscious involvement. Such functions are necessary in order for the body to sustain itself.

Since knowledge entails the dual sensitivity of attraction to good and repulsion from evil, we must properly balance the tensions created by these two opposite forces. Therefore, it is here that we find the seat of free choice in the soul. To strengthen one's nervous system is to strengthen one's power of free choice, to be clear and unequivocal about choosing good and repelling evil. In the words of the Torah, "See, I have given you this day life and good, death and evil... Choose life."[15]

By choosing good as defined by the Torah, God's word to man, we unite with God, the ultimate, absolute good. As mentioned, the inner experience of knowledge is union. It is the experience of union that creates the balance between the two opposing sides of knowledge, the attraction to good and the repulsion of evil. To strengthen our power of free choice, and thereby our nervous system, we must strengthen our consciousness of union with God and the Divine souls of Israel, which are "an actual part of God."[16]

"Crowning" Achievement

keter — כֶּתֶר

"crown"

binah — בִּינָה   chochmah — חָכְמָה

"understanding"   "wisdom"

da'at — דַּעַת

"knowledge"

gevurah — גְּבוּרָה   chesed — חֶסֶד

"might"   "loving-kindness"

tiferet — תִּפְאֶרֶת

"beauty"

hod — הוֹד   netzach — נֵצַח

"acknowledgment"   "victory"

yesod — יְסוֹד

"foundation"

malchut — מַלְכוּת

"kingdom"

In order for our expanded version of the mindsets diagram to be complete, we need to relate to the *sefirah* which is positioned above intellect on the

Kabbalistic Tree of Life—the *sefirah* of *keter* "crown"
(כֶּתֶר). Although this is, in fact, the first of the *sefirot*,
we are examining it last, which reminds us of the
principle taught in Kabbalah that "the end is wedged
in the beginning."[17]

While this is the stage that begins it all, at times it is
easier to appreciate after an examination of the
subsequent levels, which all derive from *keter*, the
source of all super-conscious experience. *Keter* which
means "crown" evokes a sense of the sublime Divine
energy that hovers just above creation—beyond
reason and understanding—encompassing the
universe while eluding our awareness at the same
time.

Keter is divided into two major substrates referred to
in Kabbalah as "the Ancient of Days" (*Atik Yomin*—
עַתִּיק יוֹמִין) and "the Elongated Countenance" (*Arich
Anpin*—אֲרִיךְ אַנְפִּין). In the terminology of Chassidut,
these two manifestations of crown are synonymous
with the super-conscious powers of pleasure
(*ta'anug*—תַּעֲנוּג) and will (*ratzon*—רָצוֹן). Pleasure
further divides into two derivative states (simple
and composite) which, in turn, translate into the two
identified properties of super-conscious experience:
simple faith (*emunah*—אֱמוּנָה) and composite pleasure
(i.e., pleasure of experiencing something outside of

itself, for example, the pleasure that comes with the experience of a new flash of insight). Faith is the totally simple and unstructured super-conscious state whereby the soul remains completely submerged within its Divine Root (and as such intuits, as it were, the pleasure inherent in the essence of its own being), while composite pleasure is the soul experiencing the texture of the soul's other capacities and powers.

Let us now briefly expound upon each of these super-conscious properties—faith, pleasure and will—which comprise the full spectrum of surrounding powers of the soul.

Faith

The supreme head of *keter*—faith—resides at the hidden juncture where the soul clings to its source in Divine Essence (*atzmut*—עַצְמוּת). It is this rooting within God's essence that endows the soul with eternal life, as suggested by the Torah statement: "You who cling to *Havayah*, your God, are alive all of you this day,"[18] alluding to the unending day of eternity.

The state of pleasure associated with faith is completely simple, meaning that it is entirely abstract and unstructured, void of even super-conscious sensation. It refers to a state which is not as much pleasure as anticipation of the ultimate pleasure that we will derive in days to come from the revelation of the absolute origin of all things within Divinity. Consequently, the super-conscious state of faith in the soul gives rise to both a deeply ingrained belief in our origins as well as a concomitant faith in the destiny of creation. The mutual embrace of both these parameters endows all the subsequent powers of the soul with a foundation of belief in the underlying unity of existence, in spite of the apparently unavoidable antagonism and conflict that marks the encounter between the infinite and the finite.

Having its root in the inscrutable realm of Divine Essence, the essential state of faith is one that cannot be grasped through logic or reason. Nevertheless, various characteristics of the Jewish soul—such as its capacity to sustain the paradoxes of existence, or its willingness to sacrifice life for the sake of faith— point to its super-rational force. The capacity to transcend the limitations of the mind and body derives from the soul's connection through faith to the Divine Essence that generates the ultimate paradox of creation: the emergence of finite reality from God's infinite being.

Since this is the simple, undifferentiated realm of the super-conscious, there are no conflicts or dilemmas over which method to use while praising. As faith is simple and uncomplicated, so too is the praise at this level. The reason a student expends effort is because he believes that the goal is an attainable one. In order to instruct a student at the level of *keter*, the educator should learn how to focus and clarify the student's belief system. If something good was achieved, then the educator should praise the student that he must have expressed his faith well, or that he must have prayed well. The educator's message is that, while it is good to achieve one's goal, the original/inner reason for pursuing a goal relates to the Divine Source behind each goal.

The clearest way to praise at this highest level of the *sefirot* is to orient the praise within the framework of prayer. We previously mentioned prayer in two other contexts. The first was in our chocolate bar example, where the child remembered to say a blessing—that is, to fear Heaven—before eating. This level of praise corresponded to the *sefirah* of *gevurah*. Then we traveled up the left axis of the Tree of Life to the *sefirah* of *binah*, or the meditative experience that precedes prayer.

But now we are discussing the highest level which inspires all levels below it. Since *keter* informs everything we do—no matter what kind of thought, word or deed—it is always appropriate for the educator to tell the student: "You must have had faith in God that the outcome would be a good one."

Pleasure

The intermediate head of *keter*—composite pleasure—is the base of an entirely different kind of super-conscious pleasure, the hidden pleasure which derives from the anticipation of our innate capacities being engaged through conscious experience in uncovering Divinity within creation. Pleasure implies the soul's coming to terms with its Divine mandate to acknowledge external reality while savoring the specific powers endowed us by God.

Pleasure represents the root of our subjective assessment of the world. It is here where the intrinsic values that the soul employs in measuring experience have their ultimate origin. It is also from here that derives the innate aesthetic sense which informs our ongoing probe of external reality.

Pleasure is the inner dimension of will (the third head of the crown to be explained next). If the teacher was successful in properly praising the child in our chocolate bar example, then the child realized that spiritual pleasure is sweeter than physical pleasure. Earlier, we mentioned this idea with reference to the *sefirah* of *tiferet*, the third of the emotive *sefirot*, nonetheless, the spiritual pleasure that corresponds to *tiferet* derives from this higher level of pleasure. Just as prayer, which we originally mentioned in connection with the *sefirah* of *gevurah*, comes from super-conscious faith (as just explained), so too, does the source of praising pleasure come from the super-conscious as well.

Will

The third and final head of *keter*—will—is initially inspired by pleasure. As the force that propels and directs a person toward pleasurable experiences, will is defined as the power motivating a person to seek gratifying outlets for the conscious *sefirot* that flow from it.

Although it is located immediately after the level of super-conscious pleasure, the executive force of will is more intimately allied in *keter* with faith, from where it inherits the capacity to actually suspend gratification when faith so dictates.

As opposed to pleasure—which, when void of its own inner sense of faith, may mobilize will in the pursuit of transient delights—faith harnesses our will in the service of more lasting objectives. This often results in the power of will being employed to resist action rather than initiate it, should such action be seen as jeopardizing our essential call of faith.

Originally we identified will or effort with the *sefirah* of *yesod*. But as we are now explaining the three types of praise which begin all others, we are also introducing the source of effort in the super-conscious level of will.

It is important to keep in mind that the super-conscious is not result driven. For example, at the highest level of faith, the educator is not concerned whether the student actually achieved his goal or not. What's important is the lesson of faith that the educator instilled in him.

The same is true for pleasure—for example when the child realizes that the Torah is sweet even without the chocolate bar. What this means for will is that even if the child didn't succeed in his studies and tests, but he put in a lot of effort, then we praise him for exhibiting a good and positive will. We also encourage him by saying that with his willpower, he will succeed in the future.[19] The lesson at this level is that while a child wants to see the results of his efforts, this is not as essential for his teacher.

When explaining the *sefirah* of *yesod*, we explained a level called the "crown of foundation" (*ateret hayesod*—עֲטֶרֶת הַיְסוֹד). We mentioned there that the will or effort expressed in the *sefirah* of *yesod* has its root in the super-conscious level of will within the *sefirah* of *keter*. No clearer indication for this is the level of the "crown of foundation."

It is in the merit of standing up to trials—like Joseph did when confronted by Potiphar's wife (as explained previously)—that a person merits two receive two levels of praise.

The praise at the level of *ateret hayesod*, as rooted in the super-conscious level of will, is that the student has stayed pure and holy during the tests of adolescence. This praise also corresponds to the level of "skull" (*gulgolta*—גֻּלְגָּלְתָּא) in Kabbalah.

The second praise is that the student has merited to become an "explainer of hidden things"—which is what Pharaoh called Joseph—as a result of staying pure and holy during the tests of adolescence. Whereas the prior praise corresponds to the crown of will, to reveal new and genuine Torah insights relates to the wisdom of will, called the "concealed brain" (*mocha stima'ah*—מוֹחָא סְתִימָאָה).

In the body, the *sefirah* of *keter* corresponds to the respiratory system, the physical conduit through which the spirit of life enters the body.

When God created Adam, He "formed man of the dust of the ground, and breathed into his nostrils the breath of life."[20] Thus, we learn that the breath of life comes from God on high, the source of all life. In breathing, we internalize that which is exterior to us; we inhale from that which is above us.

The Hebrew word for "inhaling" (*sheifah*—שְׁאִיפָה) also means "aspiration." Thus, breathing is an expression of the soul's innate desire to ascend and go beyond its conscious self into the realm of its super-conscious connection to God, as experienced through its super-rational faith, pleasure, and will.

Thus, a lack of pleasure and will in life (reflecting a lack of faith in the Divine purpose of life) may well result in a dysfunction of the respiratory system. To forestall or correct this, with every breath we take, we should try to "breathe" into our being a new sense of vitality and joy for life itself.[21]

The Diagram in Triads

As we progressed through our expanded version of the mindsets diagram, we examined each section as a triad of *sefirot*. This follows the order of the

Kabbalistic Tree of Life, whereby each level exhibits a right, left, and center axis.

At the level of the intellectual *sefirot*—*chochmah*, *binah* and *da'at*—we explained that the essence of praise was to distinguish between good and bad praise by means of the intellect. If an educator praises correctly at this level, then he will get it right at all the others levels as well. This is what the verse from Jeremiah which began this section is telling us when it says that the wise should not be praised for wisdom.

That verse covers all the pertinent *sefirot*: "So says God, 'The wise man should not praise his wisdom; the mighty should not praise his might; the wealthy shall not praise his wealth...'" When it speaks of wisdom, the verse refers to all the intellectual attributes of the soul, including understanding and knowledge. When it speaks of might it refers to the three emotive attributes of the soul, including loving-kindness, might and beauty. And when it speaks of wealth, it speaks of the behavioral attributes of the soul, including victory, acknowledgement and foundation; these all relate to what it means to be successful in business, for what matters to the businessman is the fruits of his efforts rather than the thoughts/ideas or emotions that precede them.

The verse continues: "'For only in this shall he who is praised be praised; in contemplating and knowing Me for I, God, practice loving-kindness, justice and *tzedakah* (charity/righteousness) on the earth; for in these things I delight,' says God."

Note that the word "practice" (*oseh*—עֹשֶׂה) precedes the introduction of the triad of the emotive *sefirot*, for the main thing is the practical application of all these principles in order that each child should reach his or her fullest potential.

We mentioned earlier that loving-kindness, justice and *tzedakah* relate to the three emotive *sefirot* in the same right-left-center formation on the Tree of Life model. Now we can add that all our efforts and all the proper praises and well-directed words of encouragement reach their culmination in the phrase "on the earth" (*b'aretz*—בָּאָרֶץ) which relates to the final *sefirah* of *malchut*.

Let us now present the full diagram with the addition of the three intellectual *sefirot* and the super-conscious *keter*:

Properties	Demon-strated by	Soul Attribute	In Action	In the Body	Praise and Motivation
Super-conscious Experience	Faithful Prayer	Faith (emunah—אֱמוּנָה) within Crown (keter—כֶּתֶר)	One who expresses his faith well through prayer, in order to achieve goals		Praising the Super-conscious
	Sweet Ambitions	Pleasure (ta'anug—תַּעֲנוּג) within Crown (keter—כֶּתֶר)	One who realizes that spiritual pleasure is sweeter than physical pleasure		
	Power to Pass the Test	Crown of Will, Source for "Crown of Foundation" (ateret hayesod—עֲטֶרֶת הַיְסוֹד) also called the "skull" (gulgolta—גֻּלְגַּלְתָּא).	One who stays pure and holy during tests of adolescence.	The Respira-tory System	
	Explainer of Hidden Things	Wisdom of Will, called the "concealed brain" (mocha stima'ah—מוֹחָא סְתִימָאָה) within will.	One who merits to become an "explainer of hidden things" as a result of staying pure and holy during the tests of adolescence.		
	Raw Willpower	Will (ratzon—רָצוֹן) within Crown	One who exhibits good and positive will even if he does not succeed in his studies and tests		
The Realm of the Intellect	Innovation	Wisdom (chochmah—חָכְמָה)	One who realizes that his insight is not his at all but a gift from God	Bone Marrow	Praising the Intellect
	Intuition	Understanding (binah—בִּינָה)	One who is able to intuit a more inclusive reality than knowable through wisdom alone	Blood	
	Unification	Knowledge (da'at—דַּעַת)	One who makes correct correspondences, unifying opposite things	The Nervous System	

Properties	Demon-strated by	Soul Attribute	In Action	In the Body	Praise and Motivation
Emotive Properties	A Kind Individual	Loving-kindness (chesed—חֶסֶד)	One who acts with loving-kindness toward others	The Skeletal System	Praising to Inspire the Emotions
	A God-Fearing Individual	Might (gevurah—גְבוּרָה)	One who is God fearing and says a blessing before eating	The Circula-tory System	
	A Scholar	Beauty (tiferet—תִּפְאֶרֶת)	One who studies Torah realizing that the learning is even sweeter than physical delights.	The Muscular System	
Behavioral Properties	Challenges	Victory (netzach—נֶצַח)	One who rises to accept challenges	The Endocrine System	Behavior Training
	Obstacles	Acknowledge-ment (hod—הוֹד)	One who has the strength required to continually overcome obstacles	The Immune System	
	Effort	Foundation (yesod—יְסוֹד)	One who grows through effort	The Reproductive System	
	Appearance	The Crown of the Reproductive Organ (ateret hayesod—עֲטֶרֶת הַיְסוֹד)	One who has the desire to shine new light to the world	The Integu-mentary (Skin) System	
Feminine Properties	Accepting Criticism	Kingdom (malchut—מַלְכוּת)	One who is lowly enough to receive criticism	The Digestive System	Praising the ongoing results of the above
	Relating to the Success of Others		One who is willing to learn from everyone		

Properties	Demon- strated by	Soul Attribute	In Action	In the Body	Praise and Motivation
Garments of the Soul	Focused Thinker	Thought (*machshavah*— מַחֲשָׁבָה)	One who focuses himself on the study of Torah		Praising the Thought, Speech, or Action.
	Free Thinker	Random Reflection	One who studies Torah despite perpetual drift of thought		
	Profound Speaking	Profound Speech (*dibur*—דִּבּוּר)	One who speaks words from the heart		
	Superficial Speaking	Superficial Speech (*dibur*—דִּבּוּר)	One who speaks words that issue only from the lips		
	The Essence of Deed	Action (*ma'aseh*—מַעֲשֶׂה)	One who equalizes the great and small by being kind to everyone.		

12

FINDING YOUR LIFE'S MISSION

Your *Tafkid*

One's God-given talents make the decision of what to do in life potentially more complicated, for it cannot be assumed that one born with above-average intelligence should necessarily become a physicist, or a person who is extroverted and personable should necessarily become a politician.

This is why discovering what is one's purpose in life—one's unique mission (called *tafkid*—תַּפְקִיד in Hebrew)—is of such great importance. In the Chassidic tradition, especially that of Chabad, the importance of having a spiritual guide or mentor (*mashpia*—מַשְׁפִּיעַ) is greatly emphasized. Without proper guidance, one could very easily spend a whole life doing the wrong thing and traveling in the wrong direction. And this applies to everyone—

including rabbis and Torah scholars—as the following story illustrates:

A Rabbi Who Became a Wagon Driver

Rabbi Yosef of Beshenkovitch, a Torah scholar and teacher, who knew the entire Talmud and Maimonides' *Mishneh Torah* by heart, earned the greatest honors from the scholars of his town. But, in the year 1804, Rabbi Schneur Zalman of Liadi, the founder of the Chabad Movement, advised him, "For the benefit of your soul, it would be better for you to become a wagon driver than a rabbi of a community."

Rabbi Yosef remembered this advice when, some time later, he was offered the position of communal rabbi in the town of Liepli, and so he declined the job. But now, he realized, he must become a wagon driver. For a month he wavered, confused, not knowing exactly how to go about it. Eventually he mustered up enough courage to visit the local wagon station. When the wagon drivers saw him, they asked him where he wished to travel.

"I haven't come to travel," he answered in a low voice. "I've come here to learn how to become a wagon driver."

They looked at each other in surprise and began to joke at his expense. One driver, however, saw that he was serious and agreed to teach him the trade. He showed him how to hitch the horses, attach the reins and oil the wheels. While he was busy learning, one of the horses swished his tail and almost sliced open his eye.

That night, Rabbi Yosef arrived home dirty and bruised. He changed his clothing, went to synagogue to pray and gave his usual Torah class. Returning home he found his wife in tears, for she had heard of his visit to the stables. However, when he then shared Rabbi Schneur Zalman's instructions, she told him, "If the Rebbe told you this, you mustn't delay even a day. Tomorrow I'll sell my jewelry and you will be able to buy a wagon."

Hearing her innocent words, Rabbi Yosef decided to travel to Velizh, where he would learn more about the trade from a wagon driver who was also a Torah scholar and a chassid. He did just that.

Time passed and he became used to his new lifestyle. One evening, in his travels, he stopped over at a Jewish-owned inn to study for a bit, when the innkeeper brought over a guest who needed to hire a coach to travel the following day. The guest—Solomon (Shlomo Leib) Gamitzki—was a Jew who had deserted the paths of religious observance and had become an employee of Count Batchaikov.

"What time can we leave?" asked Shlomo Leib.

"After morning prayers," Rabbi Yosef replied.

"At what time?" he retorted. "To me, it makes no difference whether you prayer or not; I need to know when we will travel, to know when to wake up, wash, and eat."

"...And pray," added Rabbi Yosef.

"That I leave for you," concluded the guest.

When Shlomo Leib realized that Rabbi Yosef would not be ready to leave until 10:00 a.m. he ordered another coach for 5:00 a.m. and went to sleep for the night.

Shortly after midnight, however, he woke up. Someone was crying. Bewildered he opened his door and saw Rabbi Yosef sitting on the floor and weeping while reciting *Tikkun Chatzot*, the midnight supplications over the destruction of the Holy Temple. That sight penetrated deeply into his heart. Memories of his youth, of his father, of his Torah teacher, of the wife and children he had left, all passed before his eyes. He watched Rabbi Yosef pray with earnest intentions, his own eyes full of tears, until the night drew to an end.

At 5:00 a.m., the innkeeper came to notify him that his coach was ready, but Shlomo Leib decided to wait and travel with Rabbi Yosef instead. Hours passed and Rabbi Yosef was still praying. Overcome with anguish, the guest went to the innkeeper, borrowed his prayer shawl and prayed too. However, so intense were his feelings of regret and repentance that he became extremely ill.

For several days he hovered between life and death. The count sent his own doctor to examine him, but the doctor saw no hope. Nonetheless, Rabbi Yosef remained at the sick man's bedside, fasting and saying psalms, and helping him with his decision to return to his family and religious observance should he recover.

Indeed, eventually, Shlomo Leib regained his strength and was able to leave the inn. Meanwhile, Rabbi Yosef traveled home.

When he arrived, he saw many chassidim preparing to travel to visit Rabbi Dov Ber of

Lubavitch, son and successor to Rabbi Schneur Zalman. He decided to join them. When he reached Lubavitch, he was greatly surprised to meet Shlomo Leib there. He had resigned from his job with the Count and had now come to Lubavitch to learn from Rabbi Dov Ber.

When Rabbi Yosef was ushered in for his private audience with Rabbi Dov Ber, the Rebbe informed him, "My father appeared to me last night and told me that Yosef of Beshenkovitch has fulfilled his mission. My father turned a Torah scholar into a wagon driver for the sake of one Jew. Now, for the benefit of many, he instructed me to appoint you as spiritual guide to all."[1]

Spiritual Compass

What makes this story so telling is that this person was not a simple man. He knew the entire Talmud and *Mishneh Torah* by heart, yet for the sake of his soul and the benefit of one Jew, he was instructed to become a wagon driver. Had he gone on to accept the position of rabbi of Liepli, presumably he would not have fulfilled his *tafkid* or Divine purpose in life. But since he listened to his mentor, he was able to help even more people after he passed his difficult test.

This brings us to the practical application of Jeremiah's words which we quoted earlier. A child needs to be directed to value those things that are worthwhile to begin with. If a child gets a really good grade in arithmetic, it does not necessarily mean that he should grow up to become a mathematician. It could be that the effort spent to do something else would be of greater benefit to his soul.

This is why a spiritual mentor is needed. Although mental effort is required to study anything difficult, it is better to keep an eye on our spiritual "compass" and move in the direction that will lead us to fulfill our mission in life.

THE GOLDEN TOUCH

The Crown and the Kingdom

We explained previously that the culmination of the behavioral *sefirot*—as they correspond to the mindsets diagram—is to be able to accept the success of others. This, we said, was the outer role of *malchut*.[1]

In order to explain how to properly approach the success of others, we used the example of gold, noting that when we see "gold" in another, we should realize that all talents and abilities are a gift from God. Put simply, gold is something that cannot be attained by our own efforts. We also explained that once we accept the success of others, then we, ourselves, are given the opportunity from Above to become truly successful.

All of the above relates to *malchut*, and now we shall see how *malchut* relates to *keter*.

When we introduced the *sefirah* of *keter*, we recalled a principle taught in Kabbalah that "the end is wedged in the beginning." Another Kabbalistic principle is that the *sefirot* of *keter* and *malchut* are considered a pair, as in the statement of the *Zohar*: "The supernal crown is the crown of kingdom." The first, highest of the *sefirot*, *keter*, is thus linked to the last, *malchut*. The "crown of kingdom" is the crowning achievement of all that preceded it.

But there is more. The source of the "crown of kingdom" is rooted in the "crown of will." This was the level we attributed to Joseph who passed a difficult test. We also explained that he acquired the ability to become the "explainer of hidden things" from the level of the "concealed brain" within will.

Further, in the merit of uncovering the "gold" within himself, Joseph reached a level where everything he touched turned to "gold." Since passing that test at the age of seventeen, everything he touched became physically prosperous. So much so that to ensure the success of the fledging new Nation of Israel, Moses made sure to take Joseph's bones out of Egypt, as the Torah relates:[2]

> Moses took Joseph's bones with him, for he [Joseph] had adjured the sons of Israel, saying, "God will surely remember you, and you shall bring up my bones from here with you."[3]

The literal interpretation of this verse is that Moses physically took the casket of Joseph out of Egypt to be buried in the Land of Israel. While the Torah doesn't deviate from the literal interpretation, we can appreciate an inner dimension to these words as follows:

Joseph is called a "successful person" and indeed whatever he touched throughout his life, whatever endeavor he undertook, "turned to gold" as he had a tremendous *mazal* (destiny of good fortune). When Moses took the Jewish people out of Egypt, he wanted this fledgling new nation to be successful in all their endeavors. In addition to fulfilling the wishes of Joseph, Moses took his bones out in order to assure that the Nation of Israel would be successful.

The Hebrew word for "bone" (*etzem*—עֶצֶם) also means "essence." Moses knew that in the merit of Joseph being a "successful person," if he dedicated himself to removing Joseph's bones and therefore bringing the essence of Joseph with him, then the Jewish people would also be successful. This is also the inner reason why Joseph made his brothers swear that he would be taken out and buried in the Land of Israel.

Joseph merited to reach the level of the super-conscious *sefirah* of *keter* as a result of standing up to the trial in the house of Potiphar. This relates to the *sefirah* of *yesod* (as previously explained) at the level of "appearance" in the mindsets diagram. To be sure, the soul-root of Joseph is attraction (a quality that he inherited from his mother Rachel).[4] He was so attractive that all the Egyptian girls would walk up on the walls over the palace (a very dangerous feat) in the hopes of just maybe being able to catch a glimpse of him.[5] But Joseph's attractiveness has its source not in the *sefirah* of *yesod*, but in the supernal crown, as explained related to our discussion concerning the crown of will. There is also an attractiveness or crown in the *sefirah* of *malchut*, but before viewing the attractiveness within *malchut*, it is important to remember that all success begins with first taking the bones, the "essence" of Joseph, which has its source in *keter*.

There are people who are successful in everything they do. So it is a good idea for leaders to partner up with them, so both can work together in order to make this world a dwelling place for God.[6]

CONCLUSION

Sweetening Praise

In many of our previous books, we explain the teaching of the Ba'al Shem Tov that every act of Divine service proceeds in three stages, according to the order of "submission" (*hachna'ah*—הַכְנָעָה), "separation" (*havdalah*—הַבְדָלָה), and "sweetening" (*hamtakah*—הַמְתָּקָה).[1] To explain in greater detail:

- *Submission* relates to the submissive posture of silent subservience to God. This first stage begins once we realize the great distance that separates us from the Divine. Submission helps subdue the clamor of our ego, so that the sacred silence of our Divine soul can be heard.

- *Separation* is the actual process of distinguishing between what is sacred and profane. It also relates to the discarding of the outer layers of the ego, in order to reveal the essential goodness at the core of ourselves. This level occurs when we remove the shells of indifference that dull our sensitivity to God's presence in the world.[2]

- *Sweetening* represents the soul's capacity to outwardly express the genuinely pure dispositions that occupy the hidden center of our mind and heart. This stage is called "sweetening" because it implies the process referred to in Kabbalah as the "sweetening of harsh judgments." By "sweetening," we convert negativity and conflict into a positive and constructive force by revealing the Divine spark of good inherent in all things.

Now let us apply these stages to the example of the child who ate the chocolate bar:

The child was distracted by this delicious treat placed before him. But then he remembered that his friend was sitting next to him, that a blessing needed to be said, and perhaps also that there are things more important than chocolate. The fact that he remembered relates to *submission*.

The child then gave a piece of the chocolate bar to his friend, and held back from taking the first bite himself in order to think about God, who is the giver of this chocolate bar (and everything else). These actions relate to *separation*.

The child realized that his desire for something sweet can be better actualized in the sweet learning of Torah study. He adjusted his attention to Torah learning, now that his "sweet tooth" has been satisfied. Over time, perhaps years later, he will hopefully begin to realize that the sweetness that he sought all along was better found within Torah itself. This, of course, relates to *sweetening*.

Not for a Prize

The method for *sweetening* praise follows the warning of the *Ethics of the Fathers*, "Do not be like servants serving their master in order to receive praise, but be like servants serving the master not in order to receive praise."[3]

This is telling us that even though praise is important, make sure not to work or do things for it. If someone else praises you, take it as a reason to do more in the future. But never praise yourself. As the *Tanya* says: "Be righteous and be not wicked; and even if the whole world, judging you by your actions, tells you that you are righteous, regard yourself as wicked."[4]

To adapt this to our topic: Even if the whole world judges you by your actions, and says you have a growth mindset, consider yourselves as fixed. This is because, as we said before, whereas a person who thinks that he is growing may become fixed, a person who thinks he is fixed has only one direction to go—forward.

Even with a fixed mindset, remember that everything is directed by Divine Providence. Even if nothing seemed to work out one day, it was all for a good reason. And if everything did seem to work out, don't start looking out the window for your chariot full of gold to come.

Maimonides states that at the time of the Redemption, all the luxuries of the world will be abundant. He even goes so far to say that these luxuries will lose their value and will be equated with dust. As a result, people will no longer experience delight from worldly pleasures. A question then arises: How will pleasure operate at that time? Certainly if God created pleasure, it must have some function. [5]

The answer, according to Maimonides is: "The one preoccupation of the whole world will be to know God."[6]

Maimonides says that everyone's "preoccupation" will be to know God. By using the term "occupation" which is the word usually used for business, he means to indicate that there will be a steady profit and increase. Meaning that when it comes to the pleasure of beholding God, there will be a steady increase to the point of spiritual arousal to cling to God (dveikut—דְּבֵקוּת).

Rabbi Menachem Mendel of Lubavitch, the third Rebbe of Chabad, believed that Rabbi Schneur Zalman achieved this level of *dveikut*.

Rabbi Schneur Zalman once paraphrased the verse in Psalms, "For whom shall I have in Heaven, and beside You I have no other desire on earth"[7] as follows: "That which is beside You I don't want. I don't want physical pleasures, I don't want spiritual pleasures, I don't want the lower Garden of Eden or the higher Garden of Eden, nor the World to Come. I don't want anything which is only beside You, I only want You alone."

Maimonides also alludes to this level of *dveikut* in Laws of Repentance:

> It was the standard of Abraham whom God called "My beloved," because he served only out of love... one's soul shall be knit up with the love of God and one should be continually enraptured by it... till he is continuously and thoroughly possessed by it and gives up everything else in the world for it.[8]

This is the highest level of growth, and why we have chosen to end with this teaching.

While each stage of the journey has rough patches, the consciousness of Abraham always focuses on the goal at hand. To be sure, Abraham himself had many difficult tests. But as a result of his intense faith in God, he met every challenge, overcame each obstacle and passed all tests. As his descendants, we have this ability as well.

May every educator and parent merit to teach the consciousness of Abraham to the children under his or her care, so that they learn to seize every chance to grow at every moment of their lives.

ENDNOTES

Introduction

1. I Samuel 15:29.
2. Rashi, Genesis 1:1, beginning "God created."
1. Dweck, C.S., *Mindset: The New Psychology of Success* (Ballantine Books, 2006).
2. "Stanford University's Carol Dweck on the Growth Mindset and Education," *OneDublin.org.*, June 19, 2012.
3. Hattie, John, *Visible Learning* (Routledge, 2008), p. 47.
4. Harris, William V., *Ancient Literacy* (Harvard University Press, 1989), pp. 13, 328.
5. Roth, Cecil, *The Jewish Contribution to Civilization* (The East and West Library, 1956), p. 30.
6. *Bava Batra* 21a.
7. Maimonides, *Mishneh Torah*, Laws of Learning Torah 2:1.
8. *Pirkei Avot* 5:21, quoting Ben Bag Bag: "Delve and delve into it [Torah], for all is in it; see with it; grow old and worn in it; do not budge from it, for there is nothing better than it."

1 | The Right Mindset

1. *Tanya*, chapter 29.
2. Exodus 2:13. Also see there the commentary of Rashi.
3. As it says, "Educate the child according to his way: even as he grows old he will not depart from it" (Proverbs 22:6).
4. *Sukkah* 52a.
5. From a 19 Kislev 5749 class held at Joseph's Tomb, delivered by Rabbi Ginsburgh, based on teachings from the sages. The

numerical value of "our Father Abraham" (*Avraham Avinu*—
אַבְרָהָם אָבִינוּ = 317) = "the good inclination" (*yetzer tov*—יֵצֶר טוֹב).
Thus the opposite of Abraham become the evil inclination. At
the Giving of the Torah, we became Adam, Man, so the opposite
became known as the animal soul.

6. The reason given in Chassidut why it is good to change the
    terminology from time to time is that it confuses the forces of
    evil, which makes it easier to combat them.

7. As his name suggests, in Hebrew, Abel/Hevel (הֶבֶל) also means
    "air" or "vapor."

8. *Pirkei Avot* 4:20.

9. *Gittin* 43a.

10. The initial account of creation, ends with: "And God blessed the
    seventh day and He sanctified it, for thereon He abstained from
    all His work that God created *to do*." (Genesis 3:3) The Talmudic
    sages interpret "to do" (*la'asot*—לַעֲשׂוֹת) to mean that God
    finished His part and the rest He created for us to do. So, our
    task is to improve on what God created in nature. Therefore, it is
    a good idea for a growth mindset person, or someone who
    wants to be successful, to keep this teaching in mind.

11. *Megillah* 6b.

12. "If you eat from the toil of your hands, you are praiseworthy,
    and it is good for you." (Psalms 128:2)

13. *Hayom Yom*, 12 Sivan.

14. *Bava Batra* 21a-22a.

2 | The Kabbalistic View

1. Energy (*on* –אוֹן) is the procreative power in the soul.

2. Exodus 24:10 and Ezekiel 1:26, 10:1.

3. Based on a letter written by the Ba'al Shem Tov, the 18ᵗʰ century founder of the Chassidic Movement. This subject is discussed in detail in the introduction of our book *The Hebrew Letters*.

4. The question arises whether God's choice of how to reveal Himself reflects His true essence, in which case, though we cannot fathom His essence, we can gather something about it from the Torah, the blueprint of all that exists, or, whether the prism that God chooses does not reflect His essence. In Kabbalah, this question remains open. In Chassidut, the former view is openly condoned to create a stronger feeling of the immanence rather than of absolute transcendence of the Almighty. This topic is covered in length in the article *Shlosha Chushim* ("Three Intuitions") in our Hebrew book, *Esa Einai*.

5. For a more thorough explanation see Chapter 6 of our book, *What You Need to Know About Kabbalah*.

6. *Midrash Tanchuma*, *Naso* (ed. Buber 24).

3 | Challenges and Obstacles

1. *Zohar*, *Bamidbar* 236a.

2. The first force will be discussed here; the second force, which follows out of the first, is that of "glory" or the resplendent aura of majesty that comes to a person after being acknowledged by the Supreme Higher Power.

3. The very name "Jew" (*Yehudi*—יְהוּדִי) derives from *hod* (הוֹד) and thus indicates that the most essential manifestation of Jewishness is the ability of the Jew to acknowledge, fully, in truth, that God our Creator is the unique, supreme power and infinite source of intelligence to whom we bow.

4. Jeremiah 31:3.

5. This statement is recorded by Rabbi Yaakov Yosef of Polonne in the name of the Ba'al Shem Tov. *Toldot Yaakov Yosef*, *Yitro*, *Mitzvat Anochi*.

6. *Kiddushin* 2b.

7. Hayom Yom 14th Iyar.

8. *Tanya, Iggeret Hakodesh* 11.

9. *Vayikra Rabah* 24:3. Rebbe Nachman's statement: "I have been victorious and I will be victorious" (netzachti v'enatzeach) is found in Chabad as *didan natzach,* which means "ours is victorious." This is a statement from the sages that the Lubavitcher Rebbe adopted. See for example Torat Menachem 5711 10th Cheshvan; Ibid 19th Kislev, etc.

10. From the original Yiddish: *L'chatchilah Ariber!*

11. *Likutei Moharan* II 78.

12. *Yoma* 15b. We show deference to the right side because the Torah specifies the use of the right side on various occasions. An example of this is Jacob's insistence on blessing his grandson Ephraim with his right hand because of the tribe of Ephraim's future greatness (Genesis 48:18-19).

13. Zohar III, Parashat Naso; cited in Tanya Igeret Hakodesh Ch. 26.

14. In the context of the Redemption, this is similar to Rebbe Nachman of Breslov's teaching that when it becomes apparent that the Messiah will be triumphant over his enemies, he will emerge victorious without single battle and without shooting even one bullet. *Siach Sarfei Kodesh,* 2:67.

15. Water itself symbolizes the fountain of the Divine wisdom of the Torah. Riding the inner hollow of the wave then reminds us of the power of "Divine Nothingness" from whence all wisdom derives. Appropriately enough, the word "wisdom" (*chochmah*—חָכְמָה) is read in the *Zohar* (Numbers 220b) as two words, *koach mah*—כֹּחַ מַה "the power of what [i.e., nothing]."

16. *Eruvin,* 53b.

17. Deuteronomy 30:14.

18. *Tanya,* Foreword.

19. Dweck, pp. 39-40.

20. Unlike hands which work independently, the legs walk together in partnership. This is explained more in our book *The Anatomy of the Soul, p. 108*. The source for corresponding the *sefirot* to the limbs of the body comes from *Petach Eliyahu*, the section read before the afternoon service on Friday. (Introduction to *Tikunei Zohar* 17a).

21. *Zohar, Vayikra* 7b etc.

22. The sages speak of seven fluids that correspond to the seven *sefirot*, and milk is the one that corresponds to the *sefirah* of victory. (See *Body, Mind and Soul*, pp. 106-9)

23. See Deuteronomy 8:18.

24. In general, education is the discipline that corresponds to *netzach*. See our pamphlet, *The Torah Academy*, p. 12.

25. *Kelalei Hachinuch Vehahadrachah* 10.

26. As when we acknowledges the truth of others' words, thanking them for enlightening us and correcting ours previous mistaken assumption.

4 | Effort

1. תִּקוּן הַבְּרִית.

2. "The *tzadik* is the foundation of the world" (Proverbs 10:25).

3. Although the verb for "effort" used in the Talmud is יְגִיעָה, here a more appropriate Hebrew synonym is מַאֲמָץ, whose root, אמץ, is an acronym for אמונת צדיקים, "faith in the *tzadik*."

4. This saying is from the Talmud (*Shavuot* 48a). Whereas its literal interpretation is that "the power of the son is greater than the power of the father" (יָפֶה כֹּחַ הַבֵּן מִכֹּחַ הָאָב), Chassidut reads it as "the power of the son comes from the power of the father."

5. Malachi 3:18.

6. *Chagigah*, 9b.

7. *Tanya*, chapter 15.

8. Proverbs 24:16.

9. *Kuntres Acharon* 4 (157a).

10. See *Tur, Even HaEzer* 1.

11. Genesis 1:28.

12. Dweck, pp. 40-41.

5 | Appearance

1. This is alluded to in the phonetic affinity in Hebrew of the words for "skin" (*or*—עוֹר with an "ע") and "light" (*or*—אוֹר with an "א"). Additionally, the word chosen in *The Book of Formation* (*Sefer Yetzirah*) for the covenant of circumcision is "luminary" (*maor*—מָאוֹר), related to the words "skin" (עוֹר) and "light" (אוֹר). Not by coincidence is the skin that must be removed in circumcision called, in English, the "foreskin." In Hebrew, it is called the *orlah* (עָרְלָה), a word that shares its root with "skin" (*ur*—עוֹר). Through removing the skin of the "foreskin," the spiritual light underneath is revealed.

2. As taught in Kabbalah and known especially in homeopathy, healthy skin relates to a healthy sexual life. For a Jew this means "guarding of the reproductive organ" and leading a healthy sexual life within the parameters of the Torah.

3. From a marital union performed in holiness according to the laws of family purity.

4. Isaiah 49:6.

5. Isaiah 11:6.

6. See our book, *Body, Mind, and Soul* pp. 98-109, et al.

7. Judges, chapters19-21.

8. From the writings of the sixth Lubavitcher Rebbe, Rabbi Yosef Yitzchak Schneersohn; translation/adaptation by Yanki Tauber.

Reprinted with permission of Chabad.org, "the Judaism website."

9. In Kabbalah this is also called "direct light" (*or yashar*—אוֹר יָשָׁר) and "returning light" (*or chozer*—אוֹר חוֹזֵר) respectively.

10. *Ta'anit* 7a.

11. Genesis 39:6-12.

12. The numerical value of the phrase, "covenant of circumcision" (*brit milah*—בְּרִית מִילָה) is 697, which is equal to the combined numerical values of "Joseph" (יוֹסֵף), 156, and "Israel" (יִשְׂרָאֵל), 541. Joseph united with his father Israel when he saw his father's image appear before him, and this is what saved him from temptation (Genesis 39:11; *Rashi* ad loc.).

13. Also see Rashi's comments on Genesis 37:2 "He behaved childishly, fixing his hair and touching up his eyes so that he would appear handsome."

14. Genesis 3:21.

15. *Bereishit Rabbah* 20:12.

16. Genesis 39:21-23.

17. Genesis 12:2-3.

18. *Kitzur Shulchan Aruch*, 171:3.

19. Dweck, p. 92.

20. Dweck, p. 112.

21. Dweck, pp. 78-79.

6 | Criticism and the Success of Others

1. Rebbe Nachman of Breslov, Likutei Moharan 1:1: "The Torah has power, and when the one rises, the other falls, and then the evil kingdom is dissolved."

2. II Samuel 6:22.

3. "...David, king of Israel, who did not learn anything from
    Achitophel except for two things alone, yet he called him his
    'master,' his 'guide' and his 'intimate'..." (*Pirkei Avot* 6:3)

4. The *sefirah* of *malchut* is characterized in Kabbalah as
    "possessing nothing of her own" (*Zohar* 2:215a). King David, the
    quintessential figure of kingdom, declares in II Samuel 6:24:
    "lowly shall I be in my own eyes," expressing the state of
    lowliness that occupies the core of his kingly consciousness.

5. This section was adapted from one of Rabbi Ginsburgh's most
    fundamental essays entitled, "A Chapter in Serving God"
    (פרק בעבודת ה'). A translation and adaption can be read here:
    http://www.inner.org/work/work1.htm

6. See our book *Body, Mind and Soul*, pp. 84-85.

7. In Kabbalah, the king (associated in the body with the digestive
    system, *malchut* or kingdom) is the one who descends from his
    throne (generally by means of word and command) to the lower
    realms of reality, in order to extract from them their benefits for
    his people.

8. *Malchut* alludes to the digestive system, as in King Solomon's
    description of the "woman of valor" who "gives food to her
    house [body]." Proverbs 31:15.

9. *Likkutei Torah, Re'eh* 32b.

10. Genesis 29:4.

11. Genesis 29:7.

12. As King Solomon says, "An open rebuke comes from concealed
    love" (Proverbs 27:5). The literal meaning is "an open rebuke is
    preferable to concealed love." In fact, since the last two letters of
    the word "rebuke"(*tochachah*—תּוֹכֵחָה) in Hebrew—*chet* (ח) and
    hei (ה)—equal 13, which is the value of "love" (*ahavah*—אַהֲבָה),
    the word "rebuke" can be understood to suggest "with love"
    (תּוֹךְ אַהֲבָה). Rebuke that is not exclusively motivated by love
    cannot be heard and is better left unspoken.

13. *Tanya,* chapter 50.

14. As explained previously, the example for this mentality is King David.

15. *Pirkei Avot* 4:15.

16. As explained at length in our book, *Body, Mind and Soul.*

17. Proverbs 22:13.

18. The difference between the two also relates to the way in which they both relate to criticism. A person who is lowly gobbles up criticism. If he is a fox, he judges the success of others and analyzes it because he appreciates it objectively. But a lion just loves for people to criticize him, he just eats it up. Like the Tribe of Judah, the sign of which is the lion.)

7 | The Jewish Approach to Growth

1. This is something treated at length in our book, *The Art of Education: Internalizing Ever-New Horizons,* chapter 7. There it explains that the ability to make proper use of praise and rebuke is the final skill needed by educators to properly shape the character of their students.

2. *Pirkei Avot* 1:14.

3. See *Noam Elimelech, Parashat Emor.*

4. *Sippurei Ma'asiot, A Story of Seven Beggars.*

5. Zachariah 3:7.

6. *Keter Shem Tov,* 1.

7. For instance, Michael is called the angel of loving-kindness, Gabriel the angel of might. While Abraham often corresponds to loving-kindness in Kabbalah, and Isaac to might, at the *Akeidah,* the Binding of Isaac, their attributes became inter-included, thus manifesting the essential difference between souls and angels.

8. As with the account of the "fallen angels" who moved in the wrong direction. The Midrash relates that in the years before the

Flood, when violence and promiscuity pervaded the earth, two angels (*Shamchazai* and *Azael*) pleaded before the Almighty to allow them to dwell among the humans, and sanctify His name. But, as soon as these two heavenly beings came into contact with the material world, they too became corrupted (*Yalkut Shimoni, Bereishit* 44).

8 | Five Types of Effort

1. Likewise, the name of the angels in the lowest world, the "World of "Action" (עולם העשיה), are also called "wheels" (אופנים), or "fixed" relative to the worlds above it. See *Pardes Rimonim*, Gate 23 ch. 18; *Etz Chayim* Gate 42, ch. 13; ibid Gate 50 chs. 7 and 8.

2. "The orders of the God are straight, causing the heart to rejoice; the commandment of the God is clear, enlightening the eyes." (Psalms 19:9).

3. The word "circuit," the seventh synonym for "road" in Hebrew, also represents the ability to rectify the world itself. The seven synonyms for "road" (with their corresponding *sefirot*) are: loving-kindness: "pathway" (חֶסֶד: נָתִיב); might: "lane" (גְבוּרָה: מִשְׁעוֹל); beauty: "way" (תִּפְאֶרֶת: דֶּרֶךְ) victory: "trail" (נֶצַח: שְׁבִיל); acknowledgment: "path" (הוֹד: מְסִלָּה); foundation: "passageway" (יְסוֹד: אֹרַח); kingdom: "circuit" (מַלְכוּת: מַעְגָּל).

4. Note that the word "righteousness" (*tzedek*—צֶדֶק) always appears in conjunction with the final *sefirah* of *malchut*, or external reality. (From *Patach Eliyahu*, where it reads "righteousness is the holy kingdom"—צֶדֶק מַלְכוּתָא קַדִּישָׁא). As "circuit" is the seventh synonym for "road" (see previous endnote), the occurrence of "circuit" in this Psalm also corresponds to kingdom, or King David himself.

5. See commentaries to, "I have pursued my enemies and overtaken them, never turning back until they were consumed." (Psalms 18:38).

6. To emphasize the importance of the *ba'al teshuvah* mindset—even for those who have been religiously observant throughout their lives—Rabbi Schneur Zalman of Liadi, founder of Chabad, originally considered calling his movement *"ba'alei teshuvah"* ("the movement of returnees").

7. Deuteronomy 32:4.

8. Psalms 22:7. A worm itself is also like a garden hose—a garden hose on the move.

9. Although we did not mention it by name, we actually referred to symmetry principle when we said that there are two ways in which a king rules—either from afar (when wealthy and poor, the big and small, appear the same from his perspective) or up close (when he goes out into the fields to meet his working subjects face-to-face). While there are these two approaches to ruling over a kingdom, they are not mutually exclusive of one another. Even when a king assumes a distant posture, he can still have in mind the individual care and concern for the smallest subjects of his kingdom. And, when he ventures outside his palace gates to greet them in their fields, he has not been reduced down to their size nor is he their equal. For more on $R = 1/R$ in physics, see T-duality: http://en.wikipedia.org/wiki/T-duality

10. *Zohar* III, 168b.

11. *Zohar* I, 192b etc.

12. *Sefer Mitzvot Katan*, mitzvah 104 (*mitzvat Kriyat Shema*); cited in *Bet Yosef, Orach Chayim, siman* 61.

13. This is how Rebbe Nachman approached his service. He constantly "began again" as if he had never achieved any particular level before. (See introduction to *Peulat Hatzadik.*)

14. In modern string theory there is an equivalent concept called a zero-brane. In string theory, a zero-brane (D0-brane) is a

dimensionless point-charge that serves to connect string-charges in any space-time dimension.

15. For instance, the story is told how at the end of his life, the Alter Rebbe looked up at the ceiling and said he no longer saw the beam, but the Divine Nothingness that creates it.

16. For a commentary from Rabbi Ginsburgh to this story, read: http://www.inner.org/spiritual-masters/yisrael-ruzhin/yisrael-ruzhin-1.php.

17. For more on King David, the Ba'al Shem Tov and wormholes, read our book *Lectures on Torah and Modern Physics*, pp. 159-162.

9 | Three Types of Praise

1. *Netzach* (victory), *hod* (acknowledgment) and *yesod* (foundation) are considered "behavioral," while *chesed* (loving-kindness), *gevurah* (might) and *tiferet* (beauty) are considered "emotive."

2. These needs are ultimately influenced by the intellectual attributes of the soul that reside above the three emotive attributes.

3. Also see the *Hayom Yom* for 5 Menachem Av which trains us how to "eat a chocolate bar."

4. The initial letters of these three attributes— *chassid* (חָסִיד), "God fearing" (יְרֵא שָׁמַיִם), and Torah scholar (לַמְדָן)—spell the word "soldier" (חַיָל) itself, and also correspond to the three types of emotive praise just mentioned.

5. Psalms 84:8.

6. Maimonides, *Mishneh Torah*, Laws of Repentance 3:4.

7. The Rebbe Rashab so much liked the image of a chassid as a soldier, that he even rephrased the meaning of Chabad (חב״ד)— which stands for "wisdom" (חָכְמָה), "understanding" (בִּינָה) and "knowledge" (דַּעַת) to mean "soldiers of the House of David" (חַיָלֵי בֵּית דָוִד), *With Light and with Might (Tonu Rabbanan Ner Chanukah, 5643 and Kol Hayotzei LeMilchemet Beit David, 5661).*

Translated by Rabbi Eliyahu Touger and Uri Kaploun. This also reminds us that King David was the one who moved the most from "level to level" like a *ba'al teshuvah.*

8. Psalms 89:3.

9. The word "loving-kindness" (חֶסֶד) hints at the words, "compassion for he who has naught" (חָס דְּלֵית).

10. The reference to loving-kindness as "greatness" (גְּדֻלָּה) is based upon I Chronicles 29:11, from which the names and order of the seven lower *sefirot* are derived: "To You, O God, is the greatness [חֶסֶד] and the might [גְּבוּרָה] and the beauty [תִּפְאֶרֶת]..." whereby "greatness" is equivalent to the *sefirah* of *chesed,* loving-kindness.

11. This function of loving-kindness is reflected in its depiction by the *Zohar* as the "day of creation accompanying all other days" (the seven lower *sefirot* are commonly identified in Kabbalah with the seven days of creation), an association inspired by the verse in Psalms 42:9: "God will command His loving-kindness day by day."

12. Micah 7:20.

13. Isaiah 41:8.

14. Joshua 14:15, See Rashi there.

15. See *Tanya*, chapter 4.

16. This is detailed in the Mishnah (*Ohalot* 1:8).

17. This is a hint that research should be conducted to study the relationship between appropriately loving others and the health of one's own skeletal system. For instance, although not specifically attributed to the health of the skeletal system, studies show a correlation between marriage and longevity in what they term the "marriage protection hypothesis." See: Zheng Wu and Randy Hart, "The Effects of Marital and Nonmarital Union Transition on Health," *Journal of Marriage and Family*, Volume 64, Issue 2 (2002), pp. 420-432.; Michael S. Rendall, Margaret M. Weden, Melissa M. Favreault, and Hilary

Waldron, "The Protective Effect of Marriage for Survival: A Review and Update," *Demography*, Volume 48, Issue 2 (2011), pp. 481-506.

18. Exodus 3:16.

19. The two words גְּבוּרָה and יִרְאָה both equal 216 in *gematria*.

20. *Sotah* 47b as explained in *Zohar* III: 177b.

21. Zohar I 170:2.

22. Whereas blood vessels are the container which structure the way blood is carried around the body, the makeup of blood itself has its own ramifications on health (e.g., the vital nutrients it contains, not to mention oxygen which it carries around the body). While the layman tends to categorize the blood vessels and the blood into one system, scientists and doctors clearly differentiate between the two. For instance, in the realm of pharmaceuticals, there are many drugs devoted to increasing white or red blood cell counts (blood), whereas there are medications that regulate blood thinning, blood clots, and blood pressure (blood vessels).

    Additionally, beyond drugs, there is a form of surgery called angioplasty (literally surgery of the blood vessels), and one of the most important forms of battling cancer is through anti-angiogenic drugs (drugs that prevent the formation of blood vessels in the tumor, robbing it of its vitality). According to Kabbalah, blood corresponds to light, whereas blood vessels relate to the vessels that are present to hold the light.

23. *Chanah Ariel* 2:20b. See the Supplementary Essay #10 in our book *Body, Mind and Soul*, "Contraction and Relaxation" (p. 235).

24. High or low blood pressure results from a misbalance in the contracting power of might.

25. Genesis 31:42.

26. See our book *The Art of Education*, pp. 244ff.

27. In contrast, *yesod* and *malchut*, also located on the central axis of the Tree of Life, tend towards the left. The ability of compassion to overpower fear, in line with its innate disposition toward love, is reflected in the Scriptural expression (Isaiah 29:22): "Jacob, who has redeemed Abraham." Jacob, identified in Kabbalah as the archetypal soul of beauty, possesses the power to redeem Abraham—the model of loving-kindness—from the grips of might. See *Tanya*, chapter 32. Again the inner essence of *tiferet* is compassion, of *chesed* is love, and of *gevurah* is fear or awe.

10 | Action, Speech and Thought

1. For this reason, the action alone does not always provide sufficient criteria for establishing the degree of merit or liability that can be attached to it. The merit of an action is most often determined by the intention behind it. Thus a simple physical action cannot be intrinsically defined as possessing one value or another.

2. See *Tanya*, chapter 46, for a discussion of how the holiness that is "uniform for every soul" of Israel expresses itself through the performance of *mitzvot*.

3. Rectified speech, emanating from the heart, is termed in Kabbalah the unification between Jacob, who represents the raw power of "voice" ("the voice is the voice of Jacob"), and Rachel, who symbolizes the power to transform voice into articulate speech.

4. *Shirat Yisrael* by Rabbi Moshe Ibn Ezra, p. 156; *Sefer Hayashar* by Rabeinu Tam, Gate 13—cited in the *Shlah* 69:1 and in the Alshich on *Haazinu*.

5. *Bava Batra* 10a.

6. Dweck, p. 175.

11 | Praising Intelligence

1. Jeremiah 9:22-23.

2. As in the teaching of Rabbi Schneur Zalman of Liadi that the mind should rule or govern over the heart (*Tanya* ch. 12).

3. As as in the verse where Moses nullifies himself before Israel: "What are we [Aaron and I] that you murmur against us!" (Exodus 16:7).

4. As the *Zohar* states: "Israel, the Torah and the Holy One Blessed Be He are One." *Tanya* ch. 4 and at the beginning of ch. 23 cites this statement in the name of the *Zohar* and in *Likutei Torah*, on *Nitzavim* cites looking at the *Zohar Parashat Shlach* 60:71 (See also *Zohar Chadash* I 24:1). And from *Tikunei Zohar*, *Tikun* 6 and *Tikun* 22.

5. "Functionally, bone marrow should be considered an organ system living inside the bone. The bone marrow system is located throughout the body in the inner portion of the skeletal system." M.D. Michael J. Sarg, M.A. Ann D. Gross, *The Cancer Dictionary: An A-to-Z Guide to more than 2500 Terms*. Facts on File, 3rd Edition, 2007, p. 39.

6. Psalms 104:24.

7. *Chagigah* 14a.

8. The most common Scriptural expression applied to the *sefirah* of *binah* is Psalms 113:9: "the mother of children does rejoice." The identification of *binah* with the mother follows from an hermeneutic interpretation of Proverbs 2:3: "'If you call out for understanding'—do not read 'if' (אם) but rather 'mother' (אֵם)," implying that the verse reads "and you shall call understanding 'mother.'" *Zohar* II 201:1; Ibid 177:2; *Zohar* III 290:1 etc.

9. *Nidah* 31a.

10. Psalms 113:9.

11. For instance, dozens of studies have been conducted that correlate cerebral blood flow abnormalities to an unhealthy states of mind.

12. Furthermore, although not explicitly stated, we have derived from the following statement of the sages from Nidah 31a (also sourced in fn. 174) that the white blood cells are from the father, and the red blood cells from the mother: "His father supplies the white seed, out of which are formed the child's bones, sinews, nails, the brain in his head, and the white in his eye. His mother supplies the red seed, out of which is formed his skin, flesh, hair, blood and the black of his eye." According to the literal reading, we learn that blood is from the mother since its final appearance is red (even though it contains both white and red blood cells); therefore we took the liberty to subdivide further on our own.

13. See *Etz Chaim* 25b.

14. While still enclothed within *keter*, this force expresses itself as the super-conscious power to endure the fundamental paradoxes of existence. When it descends into the *sefirah* of *da'at*, it manifests as the capacity to both bind together (or unify) the conscious powers of *chochmah* and *binah* as well as bridge the opposing domains of the intellect and the emotive character attributes in the soul.

15. Deuteronomy 30:19.

16. Job 31:2; *Tanya,* chapter 2.

17. *Sefer Yetzirah* 1:6.

18. Deuteronomy 4:4.

19. As the sages teach, "nothing stands before (the force of one's) will," and "there is nothing as forceful as will."

20. Genesis 2:7.

21. Our breathing meditation can be found here: http://www.inner.org/meditate/default.htm

12 | Finding Your Life's Mission

1. From the introduction to the book *Pokei'ach Ivrim*. Adapted by Rabbi Shimon Hellinger in *Lmaan Yishmeu*, a weekly newsletter by *Merkaz Anash* (www.MerkazAnash.com). Used with permission.

The Golden Touch

1. Whereas the inner role of *malchut* related to being lowly enough to accept criticism from others.

2. Earlier we said that Moses was the one who nullified himself before God and Israel. In Kabbalah, Moses is the archetypical soul of the *sefirah* of *chochmah*, whose inner experience is nullification as explained there. At first glance, it would seem that another *tzadik* could not be on a higher level than Moses and the *sefirah* of *chochmah* that he represents. However, Kabbalah suggests that Joseph was, in fact, on a higher level.

3. Exodus 13:19.

4. Joseph was beautiful (Genesis 39:6) like his mother Rachel (Genesis 29:17).

5. "The women of Egypt strode out on the wall to gaze upon his beauty. Of the women, each one strode to a place from which she could catch a glimpse of him." *Rashi* on Genesis 49:22.

6. As mentioned above (fn.189), Moses is the archetypal soul of *chochmah*, whereas the source of the soul-root of Joseph is above that in the supernal crown, which is also the source of *mazal*. The Ba'al Shem Tov teaches that whenever the Hebrew world "no" (אין) appears in the Torah text, we can change its vowels to read "nothing" (אין), referring in Kabbalah to the "Divine Nothingness" from which all reality is continuously recreated. Accordingly, the teaching of the sages that "there is no (אין) *mazal* to Israel," can then be read as "Divine Nothingness (אין) is

the *mazal* (fate) of Israel." As explained previously, the source of the awareness of "Divine Nothingness" is in the *sefirah* of *crown*.

Conclusion

1. *Keter Shem Tov* (ed. Kehot) 28.
2. The two elements of separation—removing the vulgar and revealing the good—are themselves reflected in the stages of circumcision: The first stage (מִילָה) involves cutting off the foreskin (עָרְלָה), symbol of spiritual insensitivity; the second stage (פְּרִיעָה), whereby the remaining transparent membrane is removed so as to expose the crown of the organ, symbolizes the revelation of the essential goodness within the soul.
3. *Pirkei Avot* 1:3.
4. *Tanya*, chapter 1.
5. *Mishneh Torah*, Laws of Kings and Wars 12:5.
6. As King David states: "To behold the pleasantness of the God," (Psalms 27:4) and as Isaiah states "Then shall you delight yourself in God..." (Isaiah 58:14).
7. Psalms 73:25.
8. Reprinted with permission from *Sichos* in English, http://www.sichosinenglish.org/books/sichos-in-english/26/01.htm.

www.ingramcontent.com/pod-product-compliance
Lightning Source LLC
Chambersburg PA
CBHW021139090426
42740CB00008B/845